T0316591

Cambridge Elements

Elements in the Global Middle Ages
edited by
Geraldine Heng
University of Texas at Austin
Susan Noakes
University of Minnesota, Twin Cities

EARLY TANG CHINA AND THE WORLD, 618–750 CE

Shao-yun Yang
Denison University

CAMBRIDGE
UNIVERSITY PRESS

Shaftesbury Road, Cambridge CB2 8EA, United Kingdom

One Liberty Plaza, 20th Floor, New York, NY 10006, USA

477 Williamstown Road, Port Melbourne, VIC 3207, Australia

314–321, 3rd Floor, Plot 3, Splendor Forum, Jasola District Centre, New Delhi – 110025, India

103 Penang Road, #05–06/07, Visioncrest Commercial, Singapore 238467

Cambridge University Press is part of Cambridge University Press & Assessment, a department of the University of Cambridge.

We share the University's mission to contribute to society through the pursuit of education, learning and research at the highest international levels of excellence.

www.cambridge.org
Information on this title: www.cambridge.org/9781009214643

DOI: 10.1017/9781009214612

First published 2023

A catalogue record for this publication is available from the British Library.

ISBN 978-1-009-21464-3 Paperback
ISSN 2632-3427 (online)
ISSN 2632-3419 (print)

Early Tang China and the World, 618–750 CE

Elements in the Global Middle Ages

DOI: 10.1017/9781009214612
First published online: May 2023

Shao-yun Yang
Denison University
Author for correspondence: Shao-yun Yang, yangs@denison.edu

Abstract: For about half a century, the Tang dynasty has held a reputation as the most "cosmopolitan" period in Chinese history, marked by unsurpassed openness to foreign peoples and cultures and active promotion of international trade. Heavily influenced by Western liberal ideals and contemporary China's own self-fashioning efforts, this glamorous image of the Tang calls for some critical reexamination. This Element presents a broad and revisionist analysis of early Tang China's relations with the rest of the Eurasian world and argues that idealizing the Tang as exceptionally "cosmopolitan" limits our ability to think both critically and globally about its actions and policies as an empire.

Keywords: Tang dynasty, foreign relations, China and Inner Asia, Chinese empire, cosmopolitanism

ISBNs: 9781009214643 (PB), 9781009214612 (OC)
ISSNs: 2632–3427 (online), 2632–3419 (print)

Contents

Introduction

In April or May 630 CE, numerous foreign rulers came to the court of the Tang emperor, Taizong (Li Shimin,[1] r. 626–49), in the city of Chang'an (Xi'an, Shaanxi), kowtowed in homage, and asked him to accept the title "Celestial Khagan" (*tian kehan*).[2] According to sources written in the ninth and tenth centuries, Taizong responded by asking his assembled ministers, "I am the Son of Heaven of the Great Tang; should I now also play the lesser role of a khagan?" The ministers and foreign rulers greeted this assertion of Chinese superiority with cries of *wansui* ("10,000 years"), effectively "long live the emperor!" Thenceforth, Taizong's edicts to vassal rulers in "the Western Regions and the far northern wastes" – that is, Central Asia and the Mongolian steppe – were purportedly all signed "the Emperor and Celestial Khagan" (*huangdi tian kehan*). When a foreign ruler or chieftain died, Taizong would issue an edict investing his heir with the legitimate right to rule. "Thus," the sources claim, "began our dominance over the barbarians of the world's four quarters."[3]

"Celestial Khagan" was a hybrid title. The Sinitic *tian* (celestial, heavenly) was probably a translation of *Tengri*, the supreme celestial god of the steppe peoples. It thus carried connotations of sacral kingship similar to a traditional title used by Chinese emperors, "Son of Heaven" (*tianzi*). Taizong's adoption of the Turkic title *khagan* (cognate with the Mongol *khan*) signified an assumption of suzerainty over peoples and states who had, until recently, been vassals to the khagans of the Eastern Türks and Western Türks.[4] It also signaled a sudden rise in the international status of the Tang dynasty, whose founder Gaozu (Li Yuan, r. 618–26) had himself accepted vassalage under the Eastern Türk khagan in exchange for military support during his successful bid to replace the Sui dynasty (581–618). The power vacuum left by the near simultaneous collapse of the Eastern Türk and Western Türk khaganates in 627–30 now presented a window of opportunity for the Tang to project

---

[1] Tang emperors are typically known by their posthumous ancestral temple names (e.g., Taizong, literally "great ancestor"). I will follow this convention but also supply each emperor's given name on first mention. Numerous emperors changed their names at least once; I will opt for the name that an emperor used at the time of his death.

[2] The Turkic title *khagan* is also often transliterated as *qaghan* or *qaǧan*. Tian kehan is often translated differently as "Heavenly Khagan."

[3] *TD* 200.5494; *THY* 73.1312, 100.1796; *ZZTJ* 193.6073. The common source for all extant accounts of this event is most likely the lost *Huiyao* by Su Mian (734–805), which probably did not provide an exact date, leading later accounts to date the event variously to April 20, May 19, and May 20, 630. One of the *Tang huiyao* versions even seems to misdate it to 631.

[4] Skaff, *Sui-Tang China*, 119–22.

political influence into Mongolia and Central Asia, creating an empire that straddled the East Asian and Inner Asian worlds.[5]

For about half a century, the Tang has acquired a reputation as the most "cosmopolitan" period in Chinese history. Textbook narratives frequently portray the early Tang as a time when territorial expansion and unrestricted long-distance trade imbued Chinese civilization with an open-minded, inclusive "cosmopolitan" ethos that both welcomed and attracted people from every corner of Eurasia. Such narratives tend to glamorize the capital city Chang'an, in particular, as a predecessor to modern global cities: a great cosmopolis and hub of cross-cultural exchange and early globalization, filled with all manner of foreign expatriates, fashions, foodways, religions, entertainments, art forms, and luxury imports.[6] This glamorous image has been heavily influenced by Western liberal ideals and contemporary China's own self-fashioning efforts, but to what extent is it grounded in historical reality? Any informed answer to that question must first acknowledge that the character of early Tang foreign relations arose in a historical context shaped by multiple factors: the complex legacy of the dynasty's immediate predecessor, the Sui; the fall of the once-mighty Turkic khaganates; and the rise of the Tibetan empire, which became the Tang's most formidable enemy. The analysis presented in this Element will use these factors as a framework for explaining both the Tang's successes at empire-building in 630–68 and its subsequent phase of territorial losses and retrenchment before imperial frontiers stabilized in the period 700–50. The first six sections are structured as a diachronic narrative of the geopolitics of the Sui–Tang transition and the early Tang's wars in Northeast Asia and Inner Asia. The last two sections turn to southern frontiers, maritime trade, and the wider Buddhist world. The Conclusion will return to the question of cosmopolitanism and explain why idealizing the Tang as exceptionally "cosmopolitan" limits our ability to think both critically and globally about its actions and policies as an empire.

1 The Fall of the Sui Dynasty

In 609 CE, the Sui dynasty was at the height of its power. Twenty years earlier, it had conquered its rival in south China, the Chen (557–89), and built the first Chinese empire to encompass both north and south in nearly three centuries.

---

[5] For the purposes of this Element, I define Central Asia as encompassing the modern states of Kazakhstan, Turkmenistan, Uzbekistan, Tajikistan, Kyrgyzstan, and Afghanistan, as well as the Chinese-ruled region of Xinjiang. "Inner Asia" includes Central Asia plus Mongolia, Inner Mongolia, Tibet, and Qinghai (Amdo).

[6] For examples and analysis of the origins of this image of the Tang, see Yang, "Tang 'Cosmopolitanism.'"

The second Sui emperor, Yangdi (Yang Guang, r. 604–18), had 46 million registered taxpaying subjects, dispersed across 190 commanderies and 1,255 counties.[7] The Grand Canal project, when completed in 611, would connect the Yellow and Yangzi rivers for the first time in history, allowing rice from the Yangzi delta to be transported north to feed the burgeoning population of the newly built eastern capital at Luoyang, as well as supply imperial armies on campaign.[8] Trade with the city-states of Central Asia was reportedly booming, due partly to generous subsidies that the Sui imperial court had begun offering to merchants from Sogdiana, the leading traders along the routes that historians now call (oversimplistically) the Silk Road.[9]

The Sui empire had also just expanded into the northeastern part of the Tibetan plateau and the eastern fringes of Central Asia through military campaigns against the *Tuygun (Ch. Tuyuhun)[10] khaganate and the Sogdian-ruled state of Yiwu (Hami/Kumul, Xinjiang), establishing four new commanderies as penal colonies in the Tuygun lands (Figure 1).[11] In the summer of 609, Yangdi went on a triumphant tour of his newly conquered territory, where he held a grand banquet for the visiting rulers of more than twenty Central Asian states.

Just five years later, however, the Sui empire was on the brink of collapsing under a wave of armed revolts. The roots of this calamity can be found in Yangdi's decision, made in 610, to pursue the conquest of the Goguryeo (Koguryŏ, Ch. Gaogouli) kingdom. In the early fourth century, Goguryeo had expanded from the Yalu River basin to conquer the Chinese commandery of Lelang in the Taedong River basin of north Korea. By the fifth century it had grown into a regional military power, dominating southern Manchuria and north

---

[7] The commanderies (*jun*) had previously been called prefectures (*zhou*) in 583–607. The Tang dynasty reverted to calling them prefectures. The numbers stated here are from *ZZTJ* 181.5645 and Wei *et al.*, *Suishu*, 29.808. Note that the Sui emperors, unlike Tang emperors, are known to historians by their posthumous honorific names rather than temple names. The posthumous honorific *Yangdi* was given by the Tang court and literally means "fiery emperor" but, according to classical naming conventions, carries strong condemnation of him for being self-indulgent, tyrannical, and heedless of ritual propriety.

[8] On the Luoyang and Grand Canal projects, see Xiong, *Emperor Yang*, 75–93.

[9] On the Sogdian people, see the excellent online exhibition by the Smithsonian Institution, The Sogdians: Influencers on the Silk Roads, at https://sogdians.si.edu. On the origins and flaws of the Silk Road concept, see Levi, *The Bukharan Crisis*, 37–69. Levi critiques some recent treatments of Silk Road history and calls for a less Sinocentric approach that "moves beyond portraying caravan traders as simply mediators in China's westward trade."

[10] Many of the non-Sinitic ethnonyms, names, and titles mentioned in this Element are known in the historical record only by Sinitic transliterations. I have provided reconstructions of the original terms where possible, but many are conjectural. Conjectural reconstructions are marked with an asterisk on first appearance. Modern Mandarin readings of the transliterations are provided in parentheses.

[11] Yiwu was also annexed as a commandery in 610. On the earlier history of the Tuygun khaganate, see Pan, "Locating Advantages."

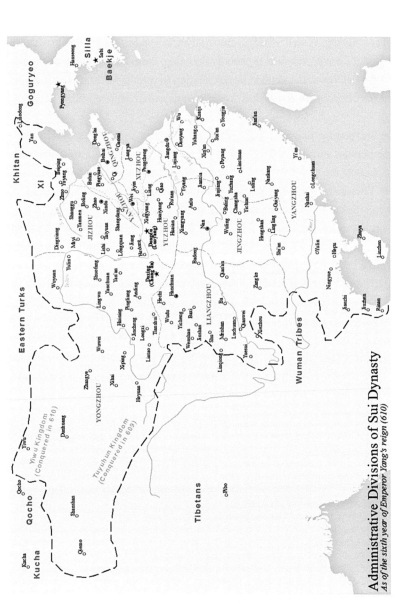

Figure 1 Map of the Sui empire in 610, showing the five new commanderies (Heyuan, Xihai, Shanshan, Qiemo, and Yiwu) established in 609–10. (Source: Wikimedia Commons)

Korea from its capital in the former Chinese colonial city of Pyongyang. A Sui invasion of Goguryeo in 598, during the reign of Yangdi's father Wendi (Yang Jian, r. 581–604), had failed miserably due to inept planning. But the imperialistic architect of Yangdi's Central Asia policy, Pei Shiju (547–627), convinced him that the reunification of the Chinese world was incomplete without the lost commandery in Korea.[12] Staking his reputation on this project, Yangdi launched three more invasions of Goguryeo, in 612, 613, and 614, and spent each campaign on the front lines, overseeing sieges of the strategically vital Goguryeo fortresses in the Liaodong region.[13]

The first Goguryeo invasion was a debacle for the Sui, with about 300,000 expeditionary troops killed, captured, or missing due to tactical incompetence and inadequate logistics.[14] The second campaign was aborted when a disgruntled Sui general rebelled and besieged Luoyang while Yangdi was at the front.[15] The third ended in a hollow victory: facing a seaborne attack on Pyongyang, the Goguryeo king sued for peace and pledged allegiance to Yangdi, a purely symbolic gesture to play for time. When, in 615, the Sui court summoned the king to pay homage to Yangdi in person, he prudently declined to make the trip to China.

The material and human costs of the Goguryeo war stretched the Sui empire beyond its limits in a way that previous large-scale projects – the new capital and the Grand Canal, for example – had not. For consecutive years, the state relentlessly requisitioned grain from its subjects and drafted peasants to fight in Goguryeo or transport supplies to the front, even while the North China Plain suffered severe spells of flooding, drought, and famine. An ever-growing number of disaffected and destitute imperial subjects in both north and south China chose to resist taxation and the draft. Many turned to banditry or open rebellion; some rebel armies swelled to the hundreds of thousands. Rather than turn his attention to the widening unrest, Yangdi began mobilizing troops for a fourth attack on Goguryeo. He then went on a tour of inspection on the northern frontier, where he planned to meet with the Eastern Türk (Ch. Tujue) khagan *Sibir (Shibi, r. 609–19).

The Türks were a pastoral nomadic people from the Mongolian steppe who had built a vast empire in Central Asia in the latter half of the sixth century. But civil war in the 580s had split the Türk empire into western and eastern halves, and Wendi's court had intervened to prevent its reunification by backing a pro-Sui

---

[12] Tang sources refer to Pei Shiju as Pei Ju to observe a taboo on the characters in Taizong's given name, Shimin.

[13] For detailed analysis of these campaigns, see Graff, *Medieval Chinese Warfare*, 146–56; Xiong, *Emperor Yang*, 54–63.

[14] In 641, a Tang envoy to Goguryeo reported encountering communities in which nearly half the men were former Sui soldiers who had married local women after being captured or deserting: *ZZTJ* 196.6169.

[15] This general, Yang Xuangan, soon went down in defeat after failing to take Luoyang.

contender for leadership of the Eastern Türks. That contender was Sibir's father *Kirmin Khagan (Qimin, r. 599–609).[16] Now, Sibir ruled his khaganate not from the steppe but from a Chinese-style walled city at Dalicheng (also known as Dingxiang; modern Horinger county, Inner Mongolia), south of the Gobi Desert, that the Sui had built as a capital for Kirmin in 599. Kirmin had relied heavily on Sui military support to achieve victory over more powerful rivals. As a result, he was an unfailingly loyal, even obsequious, vassal to Wendi and Yangdi, dressing in Chinese-style robes and addressing them as "Sage [*shengren*] Bayan [Turkic for "rich," Ch. *moyuan*] Khagan of the Great Sui." Like Taizong's later "Celestial Khagan," this bilingual title was a fusion of Sinitic and Turkic ideals of kingship.[17]

After Kirmin's death, the Sui court had come to distrust the prouder Sibir and taken steps to undermine his growing military strength – by assassinating his most trusted advisor, for example. Now, a resentful Sibir plotted an attack on Yangdi as his traveling court approached Dalicheng, though it's unclear whether he was intending to kill or capture Yangdi. The plot was leaked to Yangdi by Sibir's wife, the Sui imperial clanswoman Princess Yicheng (fl. 599–630), giving him enough time to take refuge in the walled capital of Yanmen commandery (modern Dai county, Shanxi), where Sibir's Türks besieged him for a month. The crisis ended when Sui reinforcements arrived and Sibir retreated. The Eastern Türks, realizing that the Sui army was weakened and distracted by the Goguryeo war and local revolts, began raiding and pillaging the northern Shanxi frontier soon afterwards.

A shaken Yangdi returned to Luoyang and continued planning his next Goguryeo invasion, only to drop the idea suddenly in 616 and take his court on an extended pleasure trip down the Grand Canal to Jiangdu (Yangzhou, Jiangsu) as his empire collapsed around him. Tang sources on these events are evidently biased, but Yangdi's violent reactions to generals and courtiers who protested this bizarre excursion are (if true) indicative of a slide into mental instability. In April 618, cut off from and in denial about the turmoil engulfing north China, he was assassinated in Jiangdu by members of his own imperial guard. The assassins installed one of Yangdi's nephews, Yang Hao, as the new emperor, but real power lay in the hands of their ringleader Yuwen Huaji.

By this time, the renegade Sui general Li Yuan (566–635) had captured the western capital Chang'an and installed Yangdi's twelve-year-old grandson Yang You as a puppet emperor, while unilaterally "promoting" Yangdi to Retired Emperor (*taishang huang*). In June, after receiving news of Yangdi's assassination, Li Yuan deposed Yang You and proclaimed himself emperor of a new dynasty, the

---

[16] This ruler is often identified, most likely erroneously, with the "Yamï Khagan" mentioned in an early eighth-century Old Turkic inscription.

[17] As Jonathan Skaff has rightly pointed out, Taizong's title was not as unprecedented as is often assumed. Skaff, *Sui-Tang China*, 117–18.

Tang.[18] Days later, Sui loyalist officials in Luoyang responded to the same news by enthroning another of Yangdi's grandsons, Yang Tong. Meanwhile, the strongest rebel leader in north China, Li Mi (582–619), maneuvered to take Luoyang, with the intent of proclaiming himself an emperor upon doing so. Yuwen Huaji, too, marched north with Yang Hao's court, aiming to seize Luoyang. In a series of twists and turns, Li Mi joined forces with the Luoyang court to fend off Huaji but was then defeated by the loyalists and forced to flee to Chang'an and surrender to the Tang.[19] Huaji deposed and murdered Yang Hao in late 618, then proclaimed himself emperor, but he was besieged, captured, and killed by the rebel leader Dou Jiande (573–621) in early 619.

2 The Tang Dynasty and the Fall of the Eastern Türk Khaganate

In May 619 the leading Sui loyalist general in Luoyang, Wang Shichong (567–621), deposed Yang Tong and founded his own dynasty.[20] This was not the end of the Sui loyalist cause, as Dou Jiande (who now claimed imperial status as well) soon handed the surviving members of Yang Hao's court, including Yangdi's empress and infant grandson Yang Zhengdao (618–53), over to the new Eastern Türk khagan, *Chöra (Chuluo, r. 619–20), a younger brother of Sibir. Jiande did so on the request of Princess Yicheng, who had married the new khagan upon Sibir's death in accordance with the traditional steppe practice of levirate. Yicheng's role in this story deserves more recognition than is found in typical Chinese narratives of the Sui–Tang transition, in which the Tang are the heroes while the Türks and their allies are the villains. Married off to Kirmin Khagan in 599 to strengthen his allegiance to the Sui, she went on to serve successively as a wife to three of his sons, continuously acting to protect her dynasty's interests and, eventually, pursue its restoration to power with Eastern Türk help.

   Princess Yicheng almost certainly had much to do with Chöra Khagan's decision in early 620 to establish two-year-old Yang Zhengdao as King of Sui. Chöra gave the boy-king a rudimentary Chinese-style bureaucracy, presumably staffed by former Sui officials, and nominal authority over some 10,000 Chinese refugees who had fled to the Türks. This was not the Eastern Türks' first involvement with the civil wars in China. In 617, Sibir Khagan had already appointed numerous major rebel warlords in north China, including Dou Jiande and Li Mi, as vassal khagans.[21] These warlords accepted their

---

[18] Li Yuan was not the first rebel leader to claim the imperial title, just the first who did so while controlling one of the imperial capitals.

[19] Li Mi later attempted a revolt against Gaozu but was ambushed and killed by Tang forces.

[20] Wang Shichong's grandfather is said to have been an immigrant from Central Asia, but Shichong himself was eloquent in both written and spoken Sinitic.

[21] Drompp, "Chinese 'Qaghans.'"

Turkic titles with the hope of receiving military support and protection from the Eastern Türks, whose powerful cavalry forces allowed them to play kingmaker much as the Sui had once done when the Türks were divided. Each Chinese vassal was expected to demonstrate his loyalty to the Eastern Türk khagan by sending him tribute (e.g., silk) regularly, failing which his territory might be targeted for a pillaging raid.

Li Yuan (Gaozu), too, is known to have made some kind of agreement with Sibir in exchange for a contingent of Türk cavalry to aid him in taking Chang'an. In addition, he promised the Türks all the gold, jade, and silk in Chang'an as a reward. Though the sources do not state whether Gaozu was appointed a khagan and are deliberately ambiguous as to whether Sibir was his ally or his overlord, they leave no doubt as to his efforts in 617–8 to ingratiate himself with Sibir via repeated offerings of tribute, including a courtesan (female musical entertainer, *nüji*) or troupe of courtesans.[22] In 619, however, a Tang tribute envoy received word while en route to Dalicheng that Sibir had died, and Gaozu ordered him to abort the mission. Only when Chöra Khagan threatened a raid did the mission resume. Gaozu later declared three days of official mourning for Sibir and sent 30,000 bolts of silk as tribute. It seems clear that Gaozu already intended to break free of Eastern Türk domination when the opportunity presented itself. But he would have to bide his time, as he was still fighting rival warlords on multiple fronts and could not risk a simultaneous conflict with the Türks.

In late 620, the Tang court learned that Chöra Khagan was planning to capture the city of Bingzhou (Taiyuan, Shanxi) and make it a new capital for Yang Zhengdao's Sui court. When Gaozu sent an ambassador to dissuade Chöra from attacking, the khagan was unmoved but suddenly became ill and died. The Türks, suspecting that the envoy Zheng Yuanshu (d. 646) had poisoned him, detained him as a prisoner. Chöra's younger brother replaced him as *Illig (Xieli) Khagan (r. 620–30) and married Princess Yicheng, who soon began pressuring Illig to make war on the Tang and restore the Sui.[23] Relations

---

[22] Jonathan Skaff interprets the courtesan or courtesans given as tribute in 618 as a case of marriage diplomacy, possibly involving one of Gaozu's daughters, and suggests that it was part of an alliance agreement made in 617: Skaff, *Sui-Tang China*, 195, 211. I do not think the evidence supports this reading. Several primary sources quote Taizong himself acknowledging, in 630, that Gaozu was once a vassal to the Türk khagan. But in works published from the 1960s to the 1980s, the Taiwan-based historian Li Shu-t'ung (Li Shutong) questioned the reliability of these accounts and argued that Gaozu was never a Türk vassal. For a detailed discussion of this problem, see Chu, *Sui Tang zhengzhi*, 45–96. I agree with Chu that an objective and contextual reading of the evidence better supports the position that Gaozu did accept Türk suzerainty for expedient reasons in 617.

[23] In this Element, I have opted to follow the most common Turkic reconstruction of *Xieli*, but Christopher Atwood (following Paul Pelliot) has proposed *Il* or *El* as an alternative. See Atwood, "Some Early Inner Asian Terms," 51–52.

between the Tang court and the Eastern Türks would only get worse over the next two years. Illig became displeased by growing signs of Tang defiance and took to raiding Tang territory to punish Gaozu for his insubordination. Each series of raids would typically be followed by an offer of peace, presumably on the condition that Gaozu return to a posture of submission; these offers were apparently rejected. In early 622, Gaozu did pay tribute to Illig and offer him a Tang princess in marriage to secure the release of Zheng Yuanshu and two other envoys who had been detained after refusing to kowtow to the khagan. Soon afterward, however, he decided on a policy of military confrontation with the Eastern Türks rather than continued appeasement, and the proposed marriage alliance never took place.

Gaozu's hardening attitude had much to do with Tang victories against other successor states to the Sui. In 621, an army commanded by his son Li Shimin (598–649; i.e., the future Taizong) captured Dou Jiande in a decisive battle near Luoyang, after which Wang Shichong (who had allied himself with Dou) also surrendered the eastern capital. Later that year, the Tang conquered the strongest successor state in south China, gaining control over the middle Yangzi region. By the end of 624, Tang forces had eliminated all other rival Chinese regimes except for that of Liang Shidu (570–628), who controlled the Ordos region (Figure 2) as a self-styled emperor and client of Illig Khagan.[24] In 625, Gaozu initiated discussions on a general offensive against the Eastern Türks and announced to his ministers that he would no longer address Illig Khagan as his overlord or even his equal. Instead, Illig would be issued imperial edicts, just like ordinary subjects and foreign vassals of the Tang dynasty. In early 626 a Tang embassy, presumably bearing one such edict, attempted to assassinate Illig but was apprehended and imprisoned.[25] The Türks were naturally outraged by Gaozu's temerity, assuming that he was behind the plot.

By this time, the Tang court was bitterly split into factions led by Li Shimin and his elder brother and rival, the heir apparent Li Jiancheng (589–626). In the Xuanwu Gate Coup of July 626, Shimin and his faction ambushed and killed Jiancheng outside the imperial palace. Two months later, Shimin forced Gaozu to abdicate the throne to him. Just fifteen days after his accession, Illig Khagan led a large raiding expedition to the banks of the Wei River, a short distance north of Chang'an, evidently aiming to cow the new Tang emperor (whom we shall now call Taizong) into submission. In a display of bravado, Taizong led a small delegation to negotiate a peace agreement with Illig at a bridge across the river, with a large Tang army following some distance behind. Accounts of

---

[24] On the Tang's campaigns against rival warlords, see Graff, *Medieval Chinese Warfare*, 169–78.
[25] *ZZTJ* 191.5996, 6000.

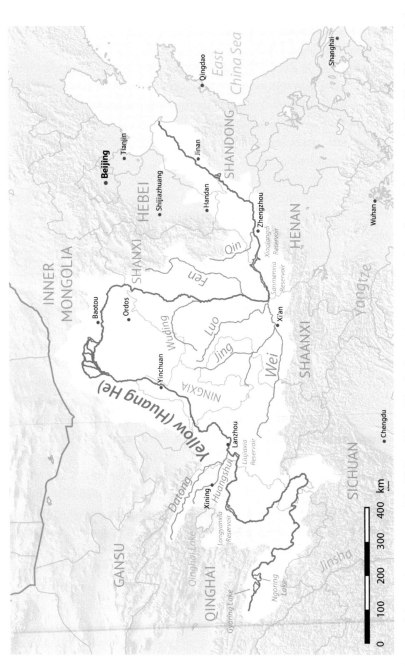

Figure 2 Map of the modern course of the Yellow River. The Ordos region corresponds to the area between the Wuding River and the great bend of the Yellow River in Inner Mongolia. (Source: Wikimedia Commons)

this meeting were later heavily embellished by the image-conscious Taizong to depict him staring down the Türks and awing them into dismounting and prostrating before him.[26] However, other sources indicate that Taizong defused the crisis by paying a large bribe of gold and silk and pledging to resume his father's former duties as a vassal to the Khagan.[27]

At this point, the vulnerability of pastoral nomadic polities to climatic fluctuations began playing a major role in the Tang empire's fortunes. In early 627, unusually heavy snow in Inner Mongolia made grazing impossible for the Türks' horses and sheep, resulting in a mass die-off – a kind of extreme weather disaster now known in Mongolia as a white *zud*. Stricken by hunger, the Eastern Türks at Dalicheng attempted to levy livestock from their Turkic vassals on the Mongolian steppe, the eastern *Tegreg (Ch. Tiele) peoples.[28] Resenting these demands and emboldened by signs of Eastern Türk weakness, several of the Tegreg peoples rose in revolt. The next winter, in 627–8, was apparently just as bad for the Eastern Türks. Zheng Yuanshu, returning from an embassy to Illig's court, remarked on the emaciated livestock and people that he had seen and estimated that the khaganate would not last three more years.[29] The balance of power between the Tang and the Eastern Türks had shifted quite quickly and unexpectedly.

Although large areas of north China had also suffered drought and famine during these years, timely rains in the summer of 628 gave Taizong a chance to attack and destroy Liang Shidu's Ordos regime. He next recognized the strongest Tegreg leader on the steppe, the *Syr-Yanda (Xueyantuo) chieftain Inanch (Yinan, d. 645), as an independent khagan, effectively forming an alliance to squeeze the Eastern Türks from both north and south. Tang armies began a general offensive against the Eastern Türks in the winter of 629–30, possibly using mobile light cavalry modeled on that of the Türks.[30] In February 630, they drove Illig out of Dalicheng, capturing Yang Zhengdao and his Sui rump court. Illig retreated west to the Yin Mountains, directly north of the Ordos, with more than 100,000 of his subjects. There, he offered to submit to Tang suzerainty,

---

[26] *ZZTJ* 191.6010, 6017–20.

[27] Japanese historian Iwami Kiyohiro proposed a more radical interpretation: Illig had backed Taizong in the Xuanwu Gate Coup and had come to demand a payment in return. There is no extant evidence of Türk involvement in the coup, though Iwami would perhaps argue that Taizong got his court historians to cover it up. Iwami, *Tō no hoppō mondai*, 26–46.

[28] In this Element, I have followed the most commonly accepted reconstruction of the original Turkic form of the ethnonym rendered in medieval Chinese sources as 鐵勒 or 敕勒 (read in modern Mandarin as *tiele* and *chile*). However, Chen Ken has recently made a strong case, using epigraphic evidence, that the original written form in Chinese was 鐵勤 or 敕勤 (*tieqin* and *chiqin* in Mandarin), and that the Turkic form should thus be *Terigin*. This position may, in time, become widely accepted in the field. Chen, "Chile yu Tiele."

[29] *ZZTJ* 192.6037, 6045–46.   [30] Graff, "Strategy and Contingency."

upon which Taizong sent envoys to his camp to negotiate terms for his submission. But Li Jing (571–649), the Tang general who had taken Dalicheng, alleged that Illig meant to use the negotiations as a cover to make a run for the steppe. On March 27, Li's 10,000 troops mounted an unauthorized surprise attack on Illig's camp while peace talks were still underway. They killed about 10,000 Türks, took most of the others prisoner, and were then permitted to loot the camp of its wealth. Also among those killed was Princess Yicheng; it is possible that Li Jing targeted her for elimination as a staunch Sui loyalist. Illig escaped with some 10,000 followers, but about half of them were captured by another Tang army lying in wait at the southern edge of the Gobi Desert. His escape route to the steppe being blocked, Illig fled southwest into the Helan Mountains but was soon betrayed by his granduncle, the subordinate khagan Ashina *Sunish (Sunishi), and handed over to pursuing Tang forces.

Even though he had not planned or even approved the sneak attack on Illig's camp, Taizong was openly proud to have made history. No Chinese empire had previously succeeded in overpowering an Inner Asian khaganate by military means and capturing its entire ruling elite, including the khagan himself. But we should not ignore the role that chance and contingency played in these events. Not only had the Eastern Türk khaganate been greatly weakened by famine and internal divisions, it was also unusual among nomadic empires in basing itself in Inner Mongolia after 599, rather than in the heart of the Mongolian steppe. This made it possible for the Eastern Türks to raid the Chinese empire's frontier areas more frequently and even threaten Chang'an; but conversely, it also placed them within striking reach of Chinese forces, while weakening their control over other steppe peoples. Still, under normal circumstances, the Eastern Türks would have been able to retreat into the Gobi Desert, taking advantage of their greater mobility and stretching the pursuing Chinese troops' lines of supply beyond their limits. Unfortunately for them, Illig Khagan had naively or complacently believed that Taizong would allow him to negotiate an honorable truce similar to the one made at the Wei River in 626. This gave Tang forces a chance to trap him in the Yin Mountains, maneuver into position to cut off his retreat, and then catch him with his guard down.

Taizong also benefited indirectly from a rare conjunction of political turmoil in the Turkic world. In 628 the Western Türk khaganate, which spanned Central Asia from the Altai Mountains to northern Afghanistan and the shores of the Caspian Sea, began collapsing due to the assassination of its khagan Tong Yabghu (r. 618–28). The assassin set himself up as khagan but was soon challenged by one of Tong Yabghu's sons. This internal conflict permanently split the Western Türks into two factions and greatly weakened their influence over the western Tegreg peoples and the city-states of Central Asia, opening the door for future Tang involvement in Central Asian geopolitics. Tong Yabghu's murder had spillover effects on Illig Khagan's downfall as well: Tang sources identify the Syr-Yanda as a western Tegreg group of some 70,000 families who migrated east to the Mongolian steppe, early in the Western Türk civil war, and immediately assumed leadership of the eastern Tegreg revolt against the Eastern Türks.[31]

3 Taizong's Empire (630–649)

As we saw at the beginning of this Element, a number of "barbarian" rulers are said to have offered Taizong the title of Celestial Khagan in April/May 630. The sources are vague as to their lands of origin, but they were most likely chieftains of the eastern and western Tegreg peoples who hoped to use Taizong's patronage as leverage over their former Türk overlords and one another. Having no way of knowing whether the fortunes of the Western Türk and Eastern Türk khaganates would revive and, if not, what would take their place, they must have seen an alliance with the Tang empire as a strategically prudent insurance policy.

A debate now began at the Tang imperial court over how to manage a large captive population of some 100,000 Eastern Türks.[32] One proposal, initially popular but later dropped for unexplained reasons, involved resettling them on the southern end of the North China Plain and making them take up agriculture, thus supplementing the empire's tax revenue by assimilating them into peasants. Another proposal, supported by several of Taizong's ministers, was to leave them in the Dalicheng area but divide them among many chieftains, preventing them from forming a new khaganate. A third proposal by Wen Yanbo (575–637) advocated resettling the Eastern Türks in the newly conquered Ordos region, on the other side of the great bend in the Yellow River. There, they would have adequate pasture for their herds and the empire could use their skill as horse archers to bolster its cavalry forces, following the model of the Eastern Han empire's handling of the Southern Xiongnu (*Hongna[33]) who submitted to Han rule in the first century CE, during a civil war within their steppe empire.

The Southern Xiongnu precedent ignited a sharp disagreement over whether the Eastern Türks could be trusted to serve the Tang loyally. After all, the

---

[31] *ZZTJ* 192.6045.

[32] For detailed analysis see Yang, "'What Do Barbarians Know of Gratitude?'" 42–48.

[33] Recent research has established that *Hongna*, the reconstructed Old Chinese pronunciation of *Xiongnu*, transcribes the same ethnonym (possibly *Honga*) as Sanskrit *Hūṇā*, the source of the ethnonym *Hun* (Latin *Hunni*). However, the relationship between the Xiongnu of Chinese history and the Huns of Roman history remains controversial. See Atwood, "Huns and Xiōngnú."

Xiongnu had eventually rebelled against Chinese rule in the early fourth century, founded their own imperial state, and seized north China from the Jin dynasty, inaugurating the period of prolonged north–south division finally ended by the Sui in 589.[34] Was it too dangerous to place another group of "barbarians" in the Ordos, within striking reach of Chang'an? Or would their "gratitude" for Taizong's mercy be enough to guarantee their loyalty? None of the debate's participants could acknowledge openly that the Türks were not refugees but war captives, taken in a treacherous sneak attack, and therefore had no reason whatsoever to feel grateful to Taizong. Another unspoken subtext of the debate seems to have been that the Türks, if left in a disunited state at Dalicheng, might head north to join the nascent Syr-Yanda khaganate rather than serve the Tang. This may explain why a majority of Taizong's ministers swung in favor of Wen Yanbo's proposal, which Taizong himself finally accepted – but with an important modification. At least half of the captured Türks were moved to the Ordos and distributed between a number of new prefectures (*zhou*), each under the authority of a member of the Eastern Türk elite who had proven sufficiently pliant.[35] But the other half, close to 10,000 Türk elite families, were resettled in Chang'an itself, where Taizong appointed more than 100 of their men as generals and officers in the imperial guards – a number roughly equivalent to that of the Chinese ministers at his court.[36]

Although Tang and modern sources tend to describe the resettled population in general terms as Türks, a significant number of the families in both the Ordos and Chang'an resettlements were actually descended from Sogdian immigrants to the steppe who had learned to speak Turkic and acculturated to the Türk way of life while serving the khagans as soldiers, scribes, administrators, and envoys. Illig Khagan, in particular, was said to have relied heavily on Sogdian advisors while distrusting his own kinsmen in the Ashina clan nobility.[37] In recent years, Japanese scholars have termed these Sogdians as "Sogdian-Türks" (Jp. *Sogudo-kei Tokketsu*) after the manner of modern "hyphenated ethnicities," while European scholars prefer to call them "Turco-Sogdian." In Chang'an, the

---

[34] On the Xiongnu rebellion see Graff, *Medieval Chinese Warfare*, 48–51.

[35] These included Ashina Sunish as well as Kang Sumi, a "Turco-Sogdian" (see the next paragraph) who had surrendered Yang Zhengdao to the Tang army at Dalicheng. *ZZTJ* 193.6077, 6079.

[36] *ZZTJ* 193.6078; *THY* 73.1314. The average size of a family was 5, so 10,000 families was approximately 50,000 people.

[37] Illig also had a favored Chinese minister named Zhao Deyan who, Tang sources claim, enacted reforms that alienated the Türk elite; his fate after 630 is unknown. The Eastern Türk polity included more Chinese subjects than is often assumed: Apart from the 10,000 or so Chinese refugees under Yang Zhengdao's nominal authority, the Tang court "redeemed" about 80,000 Chinese refugees or captives, both men and women, from the Eastern Türks after their surrender. Other Chinese subjects of Illig, possibly Sui loyalists, are said to have fled west to the Gaochang state (Turfan) rather than submit to the Tang. See *ZZTJ* 192.6037, 193.6087, 195.6146.

Turco-Sogdians would have encountered other Sogdians whose ancestors had migrated to north China in the sixth century to work as soldiers, officials, interpreters, horse breeders, and professional musicians and dancers. These "Sino-Sogdians" had often preserved their identity and culture by living in enclaves and practicing endogamy, but they had nonetheless grown comfortable with Chinese culture. In addition, Chang'an was a temporary home to Sogdian merchants from Central Asia who traveled frequently for trade and were culturally quite distinct from their Turco-Sogdian and Sino-Sogdian cousins.[38] It is important to keep this diversity within the Sogdian diaspora in mind when assessing the varied roles that it played in Tang history.

The Ordos settlements created for the Türks and Turco-Sogdians belonged to a new system of frontier management introduced by the Tang: the "bridled" or "loose rein" (*jimi*) prefecture. *Jimi* was a metaphor from animal husbandry, used since the Han dynasty (206 BCE–220 CE) to describe treating a foreign state as a protectorate or vassal, rather than imposing direct rule through conquest. *Jimi* area commands (*dudu fu*) and prefectures were typically "barbarian" client states or buffer states along the Tang empire's frontiers, in which the heads of local ruling families held hereditary nominal positions in the imperial bureaucracy, typically either area commander (*dudu*) or prefect (*cishi*). Smaller *jimi* polities consisted of a single prefecture; larger ones comprised an area command with civil and military authority over several prefectures, each under a member of the native elite. *Jimi* polities were allowed a high level of autonomy, under the loose supervision of Tang officials in regular prefectures near the frontier or, in some cases, a protector-general (*duhu*) specially tasked with frontier management. They were exempted from regular taxation in grain, cloth, and corvée labor, but might be subject to lighter levies (e.g., in sheep or coins) and called upon to contribute fighting men for the empire's frontier wars.[39] They could request the emperor's protection or intervention if attacked by a hostile power; conversely, if they aided or aligned themselves with an enemy of the Tang, then they could expect to face punitive action and have their leaders replaced by force.

The *jimi* system was not an entirely new concept. The Han empire had established "dependent states" (*shuguo*) for submitting populations of Xiongnu and other foreign peoples along its northern frontiers. The Southern Dynasties of the fifth and sixth centuries had established "peripheral" (*zuo*) commanderies and counties over the Man peoples of the upland areas in the middle Yangzi region and had appointed local Man chiefs to lead at least some

---

[38] On different types of Sogdians in the Tang, see Iwami, "Turks and Sogdians"; Bi, *Zhonggu Zhongguo de Sute Huren.*

[39] Iwami, "Turks and Sogdians," 43–47; *XTS* 43b.1119.

of them.[40] The Tang system built on these models and was applied more comprehensively, along all the empire's land frontiers and at times extending deep into the Mongolian steppe and Central Asia. The *jimi* system's use as a form of symbolic empire-building, without the cost of deploying armies to inhospitable buffer regions, is often misunderstood or misrepresented by historical maps (especially maps made in modern China) that include all *jimi* polities within the territorial boundaries of the Tang empire. This greatly exaggerates the empire's size and geopolitical influence, even at the height of its expansion in the seventh century.[41]

The earliest *jimi* prefectures were established in the upland regions of Sichuan, Gansu, and Guizhou to reward tribal chiefs from the Man, Qiang, and Tangut (Ch. Dangxiang) peoples who sent tribute to the Tang court.[42] Before long, *jimi* prefectures were also created for large groups of frontier peoples who had migrated into Tang territory. Not all were involuntary migrations like that of the Eastern Türks. In 632, for example, more than 6,000 families of the *Kibir (Qibi), a western Tegreg people, migrated to the Chinese-ruled Gansu Corridor and submitted to Tang suzerainty. Taizong permitted them to settle in Gansu, appointed their leader *Garik (Heli, d. 677) as a general in the Tang army, and appointed Heli's brother as area commander of a new *jimi* prefecture, Helanzhou (named after the Helan Mountains). Two years later, Taizong ordered the Kibir, the Tanguts, and the Eastern Türks of the Ordos to provide cavalry forces for punitive expeditions against the Tuygun khaganate of Qinghai. This campaign illustrated, for the first time, both the military benefits and the limitations of the *jimi* system: the Kibir and Türks fought effectively against the Tuygun, and Kibir Garik was rewarded for his exemplary service in the campaign with a Tang imperial clanswoman in marriage and appointment to a command in the imperial guards. In contrast, all the Tangut *jimi* prefectures, reportedly some 300,000 Tanguts in all, defected to the Tuygun rather than fight them.[43]

The Tang imperial court generally preferred, where possible, to interact with foreign polities (both within and beyond the *jimi* system) using a hierarchical mode of tributary relations first developed under the Han dynasty.[44] Diplomatic missions would travel to the court, bearing prized products or exotic animals from their home countries and letters of greeting from their rulers, and pay ritual homage to

---

[40] Wang, "Nanchao de zuojun zuoxian."

[41] For an illustration of this problem, see Yang, *Frontiers of the Tang and Song Empires*, Map 3, at https://storymaps.arcgis.com/stories/0cf798878745406fa5719b97ccfc5454#ref-n-CgqSVa.

[42] *ZZTJ* 193,6067–68.   [43] *ZZTJ* 194.6099–6100, 6106–6108, 6110, 6115–16.

[44] There is now a vast literature on the Chinese "tributary system," with much recent work correcting earlier assumptions that there was a single, unchanging, inflexible system of tributary relations throughout imperial Chinese history and that it governed all aspects of imperial Chinese foreign relations. I especially recommend Zhang, "Rethinking the 'Tribute System.'"

Figure 3 Song-period copy of Yan Liben's (601–73) painting of a foreign tribute mission to the Tang court in circa 631. Yan Liben and his brother Lide served as ministers but were also known for their skill as artists and architects. (Source: Wikimedia Commons)

the emperor (Figure 3).[45] The emperor would reciprocate with generous gifts, enough food supplies for the journey home, and an edict of commendation to the tributary ruler. The tributary ruler would occasionally also be given an honorary title (e.g., prince or general) or an updated version of the Chinese lunar calendar, which only tributary states were given the privilege of using. Due to notions of universal rulership and supremacy embedded in Chinese imperial ideology, the Tang was extremely reluctant to accord any foreign ruler a status of diplomatic parity with the Chinese emperor, let alone recognize that foreign ruler as the emperor's superior in status. As we saw, Gaozu accepted vassalage under the Eastern Türk khagan for expedient reasons but tried to revert to a "proper" position of superiority as soon as he felt strong enough to do so. In addition, the prestigious titles of emperor (*huangdi*) and "Son of Heaven" were reserved for the Tang ruler; all other rulers could only style themselves as kings (*wang*) or khagans in diplomatic communications if they wished to have friendly relations with the Tang. The rulers of the Tibetan empire got around this problem by only using a native title, *tsenpo* (Ch. *zanpu*), whose status vis-à-vis the Chinese emperor was open to interpretation.

Chinese emperors tended to use the arrival of tribute from distant lands as evidence of their moral charisma and virtuous governance, thus strengthening their political legitimacy. But a foreign ruler might pay tribute to the Tang emperor, symbolically acknowledging his superiority and suzerainty, for various reasons that had nothing to do with admiration or submission. A ruler might send a tribute mission simply to keep channels of interstate communication open, in the absence of other options acceptable to the Chinese court. He might do so for the sake of gaining access to valuable Chinese goods, which tribute missions would often receive as gifts from the emperor or be allowed to purchase at the two official markets in Chang'an. If his polity was comparatively small and weak, he might pay tribute because recognition by the Tang emperor conferred an aura of legitimacy and power that could be used to overawe his subjects and enemies alike. Or he might do so to persuade the emperor to make war on a common foe, or conversely to avoid being invaded, since the Tang sometimes used an extended lapse in tribute as a pretext for war. In addition, tribute missions were an excellent opportunity to collect intelligence on the Tang empire, though the Tang had laws aimed at preventing this: Foreign ambassadors' interactions with officials and ordinary imperial subjects were subject to strict limits, and anyone caught giving information to an ambassador would be punished severely.[46]

---

[45] The most comprehensive surviving list of tributary missions to the Tang court, including tribute items, is found in *CFYG* 970.11227–972.11252. The most influential study of tribute items presented to the Tang emperors is Schafer, *The Golden Peaches of Samarkand*.

[46] *TLSY* 8.178, 9.195. On information gathering by Japanese embassies to Chang'an, see Wang, *Ambassadors from the Islands of Immortals*, 180–201.

Foreign rulers were not always able or willing to project the image of deference that would ensure the success of a tribute mission. In 630, for example, the king of Champa (known to the Tang as Linyi) – an alliance of ethnically Cham polities in what is now central and south Vietnam – sent various exotic items of tribute to Taizong; these included an elephant and a "fire pearl," a crystal ball the size of a chicken egg that could focus sunlight to start a fire. A Sui military expedition had invaded Champa and pillaged its capital in 605, so the Chams had good reason to seek friendlier relations with the new Chinese dynasty. It was the second mission from Champa since 623, but this time, the Cham king's letter contained language that some of Taizong's courtiers interpreted as disrespectful. They urged Taizong to launch a punitive attack on Champa; he purportedly refused, reasoning that attacking a small state over mere language was hardly glorious and citing Yangdi and Illig Khagan as examples of rulers whose overindulgence in war had caused their downfall.[47]

By comparison, Japan's first tribute mission to the Tang in 631 was well received. Presumably, it had learned a lesson from an earlier mission to the Sui in 608, during which Yangdi was more than a little annoyed to hear the Japanese ruler represented as his equal, "the Son of Heaven in the land where the sun rises."[48] Taizong responded to the Japanese mission with an edict commending its ruler and exempting him from having to pay tribute annually, on account of the arduous sea voyage involved. The envoy tasked with delivering this edict, Gao Biaoren, accompanied the tribute mission back to Japan in 632 but then got into a dispute with the Japanese ruler over protocol. Gao left without reading out or even delivering the edict, resulting in a twenty-year hiatus in Tang–Japan relations.[49] This incident was later blamed on Gao's lack of finesse as a diplomat, but it probably had to do with the Japanese state's undiminished desire to enhance its prestige domestically by presenting its ruler as an equal of the Chinese emperor. The Japanese ruler may have refused to leave his throne and prostrate himself facing northwards toward the edict while Gao Biaoren intoned its contents, as was expected of a vassal or subject in Chinese political culture.[50]

Gao Biaoren's case illustrates another common mode of interaction between the Tang and other states. States that chose to participate in tributary relations could expect to receive envoys from the emperor on occasion; the frequency with which this happened depended on the state's strategic importance and

---

[47] *XTS* 222b.6298; *ZZTJ* 193.6078–79; *THY* 98.1751.

[48] See Wang, *Ambassadors from the Islands of Immortals*, 139–42.

[49] *ZZTJ* 193.6090; compare the Japanese account of Gao's mission, which covers up the diplomatic spat and emphasizes the warm reception he received, in *Nihon shoki* 日本書紀, Chapter 23.

[50] Kao, *Dongya gudai de zhengzhi yu jiaoyu*, 206–38. On how the Japanese court eventually chose to handle the delicate question of the relative statuses of the Tang and Japanese emperors, see Wang, *Ambassadors from the Islands of Immortals*, 160–79.

distance from the Tang.[51] Tributary states could also choose to send an envoy to report a ruler's death and his successor's accession to the Tang emperor, who had the prerogative of either denying recognition to the new ruler if the circumstances of the succession were deemed irregular (e.g., regicide), or conferring legitimacy on the new ruler by issuing him a formal edict of investiture and having it delivered to him by an ambassador.[52] In the latter case, the Tang ambassador would perform mourning rites for the recently deceased ruler on the emperor's behalf. As we saw earlier, some sources imply that this investiture procedure originated with the Tang emperor's additional status as Celestial Khagan after 630. But it was actually a conventional aspect of the Chinese tributary framework and was not limited to Tang relations with Inner Asian states. States tended to choose whether to request investiture from the Tang based on their current strategic and political interests.[53] For instance, rulers of the Korean kingdom of Silla (Ch. Xinluo) regularly requested investiture for the sake of maintaining a strategic alliance with the Tang empire. In contrast, the emperors of Japan never requested investiture, perhaps to avoid a repeat of the Gao Biaoren incident. They based their legitimacy on a claim to divine descent, not recognition by the Tang emperor.

On occasion, rulers of stronger polities would seek to enhance their relations with the Tang emperor through a mode of marriage diplomacy common throughout Eurasia.[54] The Chinese termed this as "harmonious kinship" (*heqin*) and understood it to be properly one-way: Tang emperors gave princesses away but never married foreign women, since becoming the son-in-law of a "barbarian" ruler was considered beneath their dignity. The "princesses" bestowed as brides were typically not true daughters of the emperor, just adopted into his household from other branches of the imperial clan. This had also been the norm with Han and Sui marriage diplomacy: Princess Yicheng was not an emperor's daughter, which makes her staunch loyalty to the Sui even more admirable. Nonetheless, marrying a princess technically made the foreign ruler a son-in-law of the Chinese emperor and increased his prestige locally, giving him an edge over his rivals. On the other hand, having a request denied could be a severe loss of face, so a ruler had to be reasonably confident that the Tang emperor valued his friendship enough to agree. Illig Khagan made a request for a Tang princess in 629, hoping to repair his damaged prestige among the eastern Tegreg, undermine Taizong's alliance with the Syr-Yanda,

---

[51] On Tang ambassadors, see Wang, *Ambassadors from the Islands of Immortals*, 33–42.

[52] On Tang investiture protocols, see Skaff, *Sui-Tang China*, 162–66.

[53] For a chronological list of foreign rulers who received Tang investiture, see *CFYG* 964.11167–965.11183.

[54] For detailed discussion see Skaff, *Sui-Tang China*, 203–24.

preempt a prospective marriage alliance between Taizong and the Western Türks, and most importantly, maintain peace with the Tang.[55] Despite the Eastern Türks' straitened circumstances, Illig presented tens of thousands of horses and cattle as "tribute" to Taizong in late 628, presumably as a kind of bride price.[56] But Taizong still snubbed his request, which apparently damaged his prestige even further and caused more Türk chiefs to desert him and submit to Taizong.

The Tang could also choose to deflect a marriage request more subtly by setting unacceptable conditions. In the early 630s, Tang relations with the Tuygun grew strained because the Tuygun khagan Fuyun (r. 597–635) had repeatedly raided Tang prefectures in Qinghai and Gansu despite presenting tribute to Gaozu and Taizong. Fuyun sought to mend fences with the Tang and gain some diplomatic leverage by requesting a princess for one of his sons.[57] Taizong ostensibly agreed but demanded that the prince himself come to Chang'an to receive his bride. Fuyun rejected this demand, claiming that his son was too sickly to travel; Taizong thereupon cancelled the marriage agreement.[58] Taizong's intent was probably to force Fuyun into one of two outcomes: either failing to demonstrate enough "sincerity" to earn a princess for his son, or allowing his son to become a diplomatic hostage in Chang'an.[59] But Fuyun had learned to avoid the second outcome from bitter experience: His eldest son Shun (d. 635) had led a tribute mission to the Sui court in 607, only to be detained as a hostage while Sui armies invaded the Tuygun in 608–9. Yangdi then sent Shun back to take his father's place, but Shun fled back to Chang'an after encountering local resistance to his rule.[60]

Fuyun had survived the Sui invasion both physically and politically by taking refuge with his Tangut neighbors and reclaiming his former territory when the Sui collapsed. He had no such luck this time when Taizong sent a punitive expedition against him in 634–5. The Tuygun were driven deep into the arid Qaidam Basin where Fuyun, deserted by most of his subjects, died by either assassination or suicide.[61] Taizong replaced him with Shun and, fearing that Shun's image as a pro-Chinese puppet would prevent him from wielding authority effectively, left several thousand Tang troops behind to support him. This strategy quickly

---

[55] *ZZTJ* 193.6065   [56] *CFYG* 970.11288.

[57] Fuyun himself had inherited a Sui princess from his predecessor via levirate in 597, but it is unclear whether she was still alive in the early 630s.

[58] *ZZTJ* 194.6106.

[59] On the use of hostages in Eurasian diplomacy, see Skaff, *Sui-Tang China*, 197–98.

[60] Shun remained a hostage at the Sui court until Yangdi's assassination in 618. He then fled from Jiangdu back to Chang'an and was taken in by Gaozu. In 619, Gaozu handed him over to Fuyun in return for the Tuygun attacking a rival Chinese warlord in Gansu. During his long captivity, one of his brothers had replaced him as Fuyun's heir.

[61] The Veritable Records (*shilu*) for Taizong's reign claim that Fuyun was murdered by his followers. However, the dynastic histories *Jiu Tangshu* and *Xin Tangshu* claim that Fuyun hanged himself. See *ZZTJ* 194.6113; *JTS* 198.5299; *XTS* 221a.6226.

Figure 4 Song-period copy of Yan Liben's painting of Taizong receiving the
Tibetan ambassador Gar Tongtsen Yulsung (590–667) in 640. Gar Tongtsen
is flanked by a Tang official and an interpreter. Taizong sits on a litter carried by
palace maids; other maids carry fans and a canopy to shield him from
the sun. Taizong is said to have been impressed by Tongtsen's eloquence
(even in translation!) and given him one of Gaozu's great-granddaughters in
marriage on this occasion. Tongtsen and his sons went on to dominate
Tibetan imperial politics for the entire second half of the
seventh century. (Source: Wikimedia Commons)

backfired: By the end of the year, Shun had been killed by his resentful subjects.
His eleven-year-old son *Nagaput (Nuohebo) succeeded him, but the new ruler's
tender age made it inevitable that the Tuygun princes and chiefs would begin
fighting one another for influence over him, plunging the khaganate into prolonged civil war. By weakening and destabilizing the Tuygun khaganate, the Tang
invasion inadvertently aided the expansion of the Tibetan empire to its southwest.
This brings us to the most famous and mythologized episode of marriage diplomacy in Tang history: Princess Wencheng's (fl. 641–80) marriage to the Tibetan
tsenpo (emperor) Songtsen Gampo (d. 649).[62]

Songtsen Gampo sent his first embassy to the Tang in 634; by this time, he had
built a powerful empire that encompassed much of the Tibetan plateau.[63] Taizong
reciprocated with an embassy to Tibet, which returned with another Tibetan envoy
bearing gifts of gold and gems and a letter requesting a princess in marriage.
Taizong declined the request, reportedly at the urging of the Tuygun khagan
Nagaput, who had visited the Tang court with his own request for a princess
bride. In 638, the Tibetans retaliated by attacking the Tuygun (whom they called

---

[62] The dates for Songtsen Gampo's birth and the beginning of his reign are disputed.
[63] On the rise of the Tibetan empire, see Beckwith, *The Tibetan Empire in Central Asia*, 11–20.

the Azha) and seizing many prisoners and livestock. Songtsen Gampo then led an army through the lands of the Tanguts and Qiang to attack the Tang prefecture of Songzhou (modern Songpan county, Sichuan), while also dispatching an embassy to present gold and silk in "tribute" and repeat his request for a princess. Tang sources claim that a Tang army defeated the Tibetans outside Songzhou, forcing Songtsen Gampo to retreat and apologize to Taizong, whereas the *Old Tibetan Annals*, an eighth-century Tibetan court chronicle, claims that the Tang and Tuygun both began paying tribute to him after this campaign. Whichever narrative one chooses to believe, it seems clear that Songtsen Gampo's temerity paid off in the end. In 640, after yet another Tibetan embassy presented gold and other treasures and reiterated the Tibetan ruler's request (Figure 4), Taizong relented and agreed to bestow an imperial clanswoman in marriage. By this time, Taizong had already granted Nagaput the same honor.[64]

Nagaput's Chinese bride, Princess Honghua (623–98), arrived in the Tuygun khaganate in 639 or 640 and soon became a lightning rod for conflict between pro-Tang and pro-Tibetan factions. In 641, a Tang army intervened and slew Nagaput's pro-Tibetan chief minister and several of his brothers, who had allegedly been plotting to kill Princess Honghua, seize Nagaput, and take him to Tibet. Princess Wencheng's arrival in Tibet in 641 was apparently less divisive, although the *Old Tibetan Annals* implies that she was only formally married to Songtsen Gampo in 646; the reasons for this delay remain enigmatic and controversial.[65] In any case, the marriage appears to have produced an informal military alliance between the Tang and Tibetan courts for the remainder of Songtsen Gampo's reign. In 648, a Tang embassy to the north Indian kingdom of Kanauj was attacked by a local ruler during a period of anarchy following the Kanauj emperor's death. According to Tang records, the ambassador Wang Xuance escaped and found refuge with the Tibetans, who then provided him with 1,200 crack troops, as well as over 7,000 cavalry from the kingdom of Nepal (a Tibetan vassal), for a punitive attack on the offending Indian ruler, a man known to the Chinese as Aluonashun (Sk. Arunāsva?). The expedition defeated Aluonashun's army after a three-day battle, then advanced and sacked his capital. Wang Xuance returned to Chang'an with Aluonashun and his family as captives, while the Tibetan and Nepalese contingents probably received some 12,000 Indian captives

---

[64] *ZZTJ* 194.6107–08, 195.6139–40, 6150, 6157, Dotson, *The Old Tibetan Annals*, 81–82.

[65] Some Tibetologists have theorized that Princess Wencheng was originally married to Songtsen Gampo's son, grandson, or younger brother before 646. Lin Guanqun has recently reassessed the evidence for each theory and argued that the more likely explanation is that the princess was too young for marriage until 646; she may have been only eleven or twelve years old when she arrived in Tibet. Dotson, *The Old Tibetan Annals*, 22–25, 82; Lin, *Yubo gange*, 156–62.

(both men and women) and more than 30,000 cattle and horses as a reward for their services.[66]

Tang sources also claim that Princess Wencheng had a "civilizing" effect on Songtsen Gampo and the Tibetans, inspiring them to imitate Chinese customs and fashions.[67] There is no evidence to back up this blatantly ethnocentric part of the narrative, but the image of Wencheng introducing various elements of "advanced" Han sedentary civilization (e.g., sericulture and agriculture) to Tibet still looms large in modern Chinese uses of her story as a symbol of Han–Tibetan unity and friendship.[68] In reality, the overall trajectory of Tibetan history shows a much greater affinity to cultural and religious influences from India, including the Brahmic-based writing system that the Tibetans adopted around 650 and have used ever since.[69] The only lasting impact of Tang culture on the Tibetan empire may have been the imported astrological and divinatory techniques later known as *nag rtsis* ("Chinese divination"), which today's Chinese government would probably regard as "superstitious" rather than "advanced."[70]

One aspect of the Tang narrative is relatively credible: namely, the claim that Songtsen Gampo sent young men from the Tibetan elite to Chang'an to study the Confucian classics in the Tang empire's Imperial College (*guozijian*). We are told that as of 640, elite men from the Tibetan empire, the Korean kingdoms of Goguryeo, Baekje (Paekche, Ch. Baiji), and Silla, and the Central Asian state of Gaochang (Turfan) were all enrolled in the Imperial College.[71] In that same year two Japanese scholars, Takamuko no Genri and the Buddhist monk Shōan (formerly Minabuchi no Ayabito), returned to serve their country after thirty-two years spent studying Chinese law, government institutions, and ritual in Chang'an. Both men had arrived on a diplomatic mission to the Sui court in 608 and survived the upheaval of the Sui–Tang transition.[72]

Throughout Tang history, the imperial court offered future officials and rulers of foreign states the opportunity to acquire a Sinitic classical education in Chang'an, usually while holding a position in the imperial guards.[73] This

---

[66] For an analysis of the historical context for this expedition, see Sen, *Buddhism, Diplomacy, and Trade*, 16–24. Note, however, that Sen incorrectly states the number of Nepalese cavalry as 700 and the number of Indian captives as 2,000. Sen's characterization of the Tibetan contingent as "mercenaries" is also problematic, as the relevant primary sources identify them as troops dispatched by the Tibetan empire.

[67] *ZZTJ* 196.6164–65, 6167; *XTS* 216a.6074; *CFYG* 978.11325

[68] Lin, *Yubo gange*, 165–67; Warner, "A Miscarriage of History."

[69] Tang sources appear unaware of the existence of this writing system, claiming that the Tibetans have no writing of their own: *JTS* 196a.5219; *XTS* 216a.6072.

[70] Tibetan lore came to treat Confucius not as a moral exemplar or sage but as a master diviner: Lin, "The Tibetan Image of Confucius."

[71] *THY* 35.633; *ZZTJ* 195.6152–53.   [72] *Nihon shoki*, Chapter 23.

[73] For example, the Tang emperor issued an edict in 705 inviting sons and grandsons of the Tibetan and Turkic rulers to enroll in the Imperial College to study the classics. See *THY* 36.667.

was a diplomatic strategy aimed at instilling in them a sense of reverence for Chinese civilization and a correspondingly pro-Tang outlook, and it ultimately contributed to the formation of a cultural sphere encompassing China, Korea, and Japan. But states who sent students to Chang'an were not necessarily seeking Chinese political influence so much as a future corps of leaders who understood the Chinese empire's administrative institutions and would be able to replicate them to build a more centralized bureaucratic system. Takamuko no Genri, for example, was one of the authors of the Japanese state's centralizing Taika edicts in 646, the first attempt at introducing Tang-style institutions to Japan. States that sent students to Chang'an also expected them to develop a strong understanding of Chinese culture and politics and use it to advise their rulers in managing relations with the Tang empire more effectively. Some students might also go on to serve as diplomats: Genri later served as chief ambassador on a mission to the Tang, during which he died in Chang'an in 654. Another example was a Tibetan minister, known to the Chinese as Zhongcong, who twice served as ambassador to the Tang court in 663–72, a very delicate assignment at a time of rapidly escalating conflict between the Tang and Tibetan empires. According to Tang sources, he had attended the Imperial College as a youth and was quite literate in the Sinographic (i.e., "Chinese") script.[74]

In 640, however, it was far too late for the kingdom of Gaochang to use its returning international students' knowledge to bolster its security. Taizong had already decided by 639 to invade and conquer it.[75] When declaring war, he listed the Gaochang ruler's numerous offenses against the Tang: He had joined with the Western Türks to attack another Tang tributary, the Tarim Basin state of Agni (Yanqi; modern Karashar, Xinjiang); he had stopped sending tribute and also prevented other states' tribute missions from reaching the Tang; he had modeled his court's bureaucratic ranks on those of the Tang, implicitly claiming equality to the Chinese emperor; and he had urged the Syr-Yanda khagan to assert similar equality by declining to kowtow before Taizong's envoys.[76] But Gaochang's chief offense was probably this: By trying to maintain neutrality between the Tang and the Western Türks, the city-state in the Turfan Basin had become an obstacle to Taizong's growing ambitions for hegemony in Central Asia. The Celestial Khagan title adopted in 630 did not, in fact, translate into true dominance over what the Chinese called "the Western Regions," as various factions of the Western Türks continued to act as overlords of Sogdiana and the Tarim Basin. Taizong now recognized that only warfare would turn such dominance from rhetoric into reality. Conquering Gaochang would secure for him a crucial point

---

[74] *CFYG* 962.11150; *XTS* 216a.6075–76.

[75] On the history of Gaochang, which had large populations of Chinese colonists and Sogdian immigrants, see Hansen, *The Silk Road*, 141–75.

[76] *ZZTJ* 195.6146.

of access to the Tarim Basin, particularly since he had already annexed the neighboring state of Yiwu (Hami) as a regular prefecture in 630.[77]

In the autumn of 640, a Tang expeditionary army entered the Turfan Depression, defeated Gaochang's army in the field, and then compelled its capital to surrender by bombarding it with trebuchets. A Western Türk outpost at nearby Beshbalik (modern Jimsar county, Xinjiang) also surrendered without a fight, giving the Tang a foothold in the heavily Turkic Dzungarian Basin to the north of the Tianshan range. As with the Tuygun expedition of 634–5, the mobility, cavalry skills, and resilience of Eastern Türk and Kibir contingents were essential to the Tang invasion's success in the notoriously hot and dry desert environment surrounding Gaochang, though the Tang expedition's employment of siege engines certainly played a role as well.[78] The Eastern Türk cavalry in the Gaochang expedition were commanded by Ashina *Zhanir (She'er, 609–55), a son of Chöra Khagan who had founded a short-lived Eastern Türk khaganate in the Dzungarian Basin after the fall of Illig Khagan. In 635, after being worsted in warfare with his sworn enemies, the Syr-Yanda, Zhanir had surrendered to the Tang and was promptly rewarded with Taizong's younger sister in marriage.[79] Known for his intelligence and courage, he went on to lead contingents of his people with notable success in each of Taizong's foreign wars.

Taizong annexed both Gaochang and Beshbalik as regular prefectures and established the Anxi (Pacifying the West) Protectorate at Gaochang. This Protectorate, modeled on the Han-period Protectorate of the Western Regions, was headed by a protector-general (*duhu*) who also served as prefect of Xizhou, the new prefecture established in Gaochang. It had a permanent military force of several thousand men, mostly convicts sentenced to exile and penal servitude (essentially a fixed term of slavery to the state), which could be deployed against states further west or used to defend against Western Türk raids. Several ministers disapproved of the financial and human cost of such military expansionism but failed to convince Taizong that Gaochang, a barren and "useless" land in the desert, was best kept autonomous as a *jimi* prefecture, like the Eastern Türks and Tuygun.[80]

In 642, the Western Türk khagan *Ibil *Tölük (Yipi Duolu, r. 638–42) launched raids on Yizhou (formerly Yiwu) and Xizhou prefectures; they were

---

[77] The Sogdian ruler of Yiwu had allowed the Sui to establish a commandery in his state in 610 but transferred his allegiance to the Western Türks during the Sui collapse. In 630, he surrendered to a Tang military expedition tasked with securing the submission of a group of Eastern Türk refugees in the Dzungarian Basin. *ZZTJ* 193.6081–82.

[78] The expedition probably carried the trebuchet parts with its baggage and assembled them on site.

[79] As noted earlier, the daughters of Chinese emperors were typically not given in marriage to foreign rulers. However, emperors could arrange for them to marry members of the imperial sociopolitical elite, a match usually seen as a great honor for the husband's family.

[80] *ZZTJ* 195.6155, 196.6175, 6178.

repelled by troops of the Anxi Protectorate. Ibil Tölük had recently vanquished a Tang-backed rival, and he was apparently a firm opponent of Tang influence in the region. Taizong is said to have regretted the annexation of Gaochang following the raids, but this is most likely a fabrication by anti-expansionist historians. Instead of abandoning the new prefecture, Taizong exploited divisions among the Western Türks and supported the rise of a new contender, *Ibil *Sheguy (Yipi Shegui, r. 642–51). Ibil Tölük was soon abandoned by his followers and fled into exile in northern Afghanistan.[81] By 643, then, the Tang had relatively good relations with the new khagan of the Western Türks. But Ibil Sheguy had only weak authority over the Turkic leaders of the Dzungarian Basin, who typically bore the title *chor* (or *čor*). Various Chor served as allies or protectors of the Tarim Basin city-states, preventing the Tang from exercising effective suzerainty over them, and an increasingly confident Taizong was no longer willing to tolerate this situation. In 644 the Anxi protector-general Guo Xiaoke led a punitive expedition against the state of Agni, whose king had made a marriage alliance with the Kül-Chor and stopped sending tribute to Taizong. The expeditionary force of 3,000 men took the Agnean capital by storm, replaced the errant king with one of his brothers, and left with the former royal family as captives. Three days later, the Kül-Chor arrived with his army and dethroned the king whom Guo Xiaoke had just installed. An attempt at intercepting Guo's army and rescuing the former king failed, upon which the Agneans installed another of his kinsmen as their ruler. The whole Tang operation, often misinterpreted by modern historians as a conquest of Agni, only further alienated the Agneans from Tang influence, but it also served as a rehearsal for a much larger western expedition four years later.

Here we must make a detour into Tang relations with the eastern Turkic peoples and Goguryeo in 639–46, before returning to Central Asia. In April 639, the Syr-Yanda khagan Inanch (also known as *Chinchu Bilge [Zhenzhu Piqie] Khagan) had offered to contribute a contingent of cavalry to the invasion of Gaochang as a mark of gratitude for Taizong's past support of his revolt against the Eastern Türks. Taizong accepted the offer and sent the Syr-Yanda a gift of fine silk, yet the actual invasion force in 640 did not include Syr-Yanda warriors.[82] The most likely reason for this is that relations between the Tang and Syr-Yanda had deteriorated after Taizong's decision to move all Eastern Türks and Turco-Sogdians from the Ordos back to their original base at Dalicheng and appoint one of their area commanders, Ashina Simurgh (Simo), as khagan. This move took place in the spring of 641, but the plan was announced, and Simurgh appointed khagan, in August 639.

---

[81] *ZZTJ* 195.6142, 6151, 196.6168–69, 6177–79.   [82] *ZZTJ* 195.6146–47.

Tang sources claim that Taizong's change of heart was occasioned by an unsuccessful attempt by a group of nearly fifty Türks to assassinate him on May 19, 639.[83] Taizong no longer found it safe to have the Eastern Türks in close proximity to Chang'an, and thus probably also had most of the 10,000 Türk families in the capital removed to Dalicheng. But one should not overestimate Taizong's Turcophobia after the assassination incident. Excavated epitaphs have confirmed that members of the Eastern Türk Ashina aristocracy, including descendants of Illig Khagan, continued to serve in the imperial guards or as generals in the Tang army for up to three generations after 639.[84] Ashina Zhanir was a prominent instance of this, but hardly the only one. Another notable example is Ashina Sunish's son, to whom Taizong had earlier given the Chinese name *Zhong* (meaning "loyalty") and a stepdaughter in marriage. Ashina Zhong (611–75) had grown so attached to life in Chang'an that whenever an imperial envoy arrived at Dalicheng, he wept and pleaded to be allowed to return to the imperial court. Taizong finally granted his request; Zhong went on to serve loyally as an imperial guard general well into the 670s.[85] Obviously, Taizong also trusted Ashina Simurgh; ironically, this is said to have been because Simurgh (unlike Sunish and many others) had stayed loyal to Illig during the khagan's futile efforts at evading capture by the Tang.[86]

Taizong took care to assure Chinchu Bilge Khagan that moving the Eastern Türks north and restoring their khaganate was not aimed at undermining Syr-Yanda dominance among the eastern Tegreg. But he also warned that any aggression against the Eastern Türks would be met by Tang military intervention. Nonetheless, the Syr-Yanda found the restored khaganate's presence at Dalicheng an unacceptable threat to their power and crossed the Gobi Desert to attack it in the winter of 641, only to be badly mauled by a combined Tang and Eastern Türk counterattack.[87] Over the next two years, Chinchu sought to reconcile with Taizong and rebuild his prestige by gaining a Tang princess in marriage. Taizong initially agreed to the request, but later changed his mind and found a rather flimsy excuse for breaking the engagement. Taizong's ministers warned that breaking his word to the Syr-Yanda would damage his credibility with other foreign rulers, but

---

[83] The ringleader of the assassination plot is said to have resented his lack of advancement in the imperial guards; the other assassins' motivations are not stated.

[84] Zhao, "Tang Ashina Gande muzhi."

[85] *XTS* 110.4116; *ZZTJ* 195.6149. Ashina Zhong's tomb and epitaph were discovered in 1972. The epitaph shows that his wife (who died in 653) was the daughter of Taizong's Consort Wei (597–665) from a previous marriage. The Chinese text of the epitaph can be found here: https://zh.wikipedia.org/wiki/%E9%98%BF%E5%8F%B2%E9%82%A3%E5%BF%A0

[86] It is interesting, in that regard, to read that in 609–30, the khagans Sibir, Chöra, and Illig had not entrusted Simurgh with much authority because his Sogdian-like facial features (high nose and deep-set eyes) aroused suspicions that he was "not of Ashina stock." The Turkic peoples typically had more East Asian facial features in this period. *XTS* 215a.6039.

[87] *ZZTJ* 196.6170–72.

he justified himself by claiming that no amount of favor and kinship would be enough to gain the loyalty of treacherous barbarians who knew nothing of gratitude. In fact, Taizong's change of heart was motivated not by ethnocentric prejudice but by a belief that denying Chinchu's request for a marriage alliance would undermine his authority and cause his khaganate to collapse from within.[88]

From 643 to 645, Taizong's foreign policy was focused on planning an invasion of Goguryeo that he would lead in person. This plan caused great consternation in many of his ministers and generals, who feared a repeat of Sui emperor Yangdi's fatal folly. But they had no effective counter to Taizong's argument that the situation was now different since Goguryeo was controlled by a dictator, Yeon Gaesomun (Yŏn Kaesmun, d. 666), who had murdered the king and seized power in 642. Taizong claimed that as Goguryeo's suzerain, he had a moral duty to punish this act of regicide. But his true motivation seems to have been a desire to prove his superiority over Yangdi, using the coup in Goguryeo as a pretext for war. Taizong had already expressed interest in conquering Goguryeo in 641, after hearing that its king was intimidated by his conquest of Gaochang, and had declared that a combined land–sea invasion would easily succeed – even though this was precisely the strategy fruitlessly attempted by the Sui.[89]

The Goguryeo campaign achieved some early successes but, to Taizong's chagrin, finally failed to break through the line of mountain fortress defenses in Liaodong when the garrison of Anshi (Kor. Ansi) fortress resisted all efforts at taking it by siege or storm. Meanwhile a seaborne strike force, tasked with landing 43,000 troops at Pyongyang while Goguryeo's armies were tied down in Liaodong, ended up landing them in southern Liaodong instead, probably due to its commander's fear of being cut off from the main army.[90] Taizong's retreat from Liaodong at the onset of winter in 645 was his first unmitigated military failure. Meanwhile, the restored Eastern Türk khaganate had collapsed under pressure from the Syr-Yanda, as Ashina Simurgh's subjects deserted him and fled back to the Ordos. After Chinchu Bilge Khagan's death in the fall of 645, his successor launched further attacks on the Eastern Türks, prompting Taizong to order a military buildup on the northern frontier to deter the Syr-Yanda.

Fortunately for Taizong, the Syr-Yanda khaganate soon imploded, handing him a propaganda coup like that of 630. The new khagan's paranoid purges of the Syr-Yanda nobility alienated his people and emboldened three Tegreg peoples, the Uighurs (Huihe), Buqut (Pugu), and Tongra (Tongluo), to join

---

[88] For detailed analysis of these events, see Yang, "'What Do Barbarians Know of Gratitude?'" 50–55.

[89] *ZZTJ* 196.6169–70.

[90] For detailed analysis, see Graff, *Medieval Chinese Warfare*, 196–98; Yang, *Frontiers of the Tang and Song Empires*, Map 2, at https://storymaps.arcgis.com/stories/0cf798878745406fa57 19b97ccfc5454#ref-n-sFqsmy.

forces in revolt against him. In mid-646, false rumors of an imminent Tang invasion suddenly spread around the steppe, sending the panicked Syr-Yanda fleeing in all directions. In this confusion, the Uighurs fell upon the Syr-Yanda aristocracy and massacred most of them, including their khagan. The surviving Syr-Yanda, reportedly still 50,000 to 70,000 strong, chose a new leader, but Taizong then sent an actual military expedition to central Mongolia with orders to subdue them, peacefully if possible and by force if necessary. The expeditionary troops, joined by Eastern Türks and Uighurs, attacked the Syr-Yanda and captured 30,000 men and women. The Syr-Yanda khaganate could not recover from this second disaster and collapsed permanently.[91]

The chiefs of the eastern Tegreg peoples, failing to agree on who should now lead, turned to Taizong and again asked him to be their Celestial Khagan or Celestial Sovereign (*tian zhizun*).[92] Taizong readily agreed and, in his eagerness to secure the Tegreg chiefs' genuine submission to his suzerainty, went in person to the border prefecture of Lingzhou (modern Lingwu, Ningxia) to meet with several thousand Tegreg emissaries, rather than await their arrival in Chang'an.[93] In early 647, the chiefs themselves came to Chang'an to pay homage to Taizong and acclaim him as khagan. Taizong then established a swathe of thirteen *jimi* area commands and prefectures on the Mongolian steppe. This is how one eleventh-century source describes the scene, theatrically accentuating Taizong's beneficence and the Tegreg leaders' servility:

> [Taizong] appointed each chief as the area commander or prefect of his people and granted each a gift of gold, silver, silk, and brocade robes. The Tegreg chiefs were overjoyed and, carrying the gifts in their hands, cheered, bowed, and danced, spinning around in the dust.[94] On the eve of their departure, the emperor banqueted with them in the Tiancheng Hall and entertained them with the court musicians' full repertoire of ten styles of music.[95] The chiefs submitted a memorial that said, "Now that we are subjects of the Tang, our visits to the home of the Supreme Sovereign of Heaven are like visits to our own parents. We request that a route be opened to the south of the Uighurs and the north of the [Eastern] Türks. This should be named the Route for Paying Court to the Celestial Khagan and have sixty-eight courier stations, each with horses, wine, and meat for traveling envoys. We shall pay an annual tribute of marten skins as

---

[91] *ZZTJ* 198.6236–38; *XTS* 217b.6138–39.

[92] The two titles appear interchangeably in our sources. *ZZTJ* 198.6238–40; *THY* 73.1314, 96.1725.

[93] *ZZTJ* 198.6237–40; *THY* 96.1725.

[94] Compare the version in the *Tang huiyao* and *Cefu yuangui*: "The Tegreg saw [the silk robes] and were astonished, having never seen or even heard of them before. Carrying the gifts in their hands, they bowed and thanked the emperor, spinning around and crying out in the dust." *THY* 96.1726; *CFYG* 974.11274.

[95] These included styles from Central Asia, India, and Korea.

taxes. We also ask to be given skilled [Chinese] writers to compose our memorials for us." The emperor granted all these requests.

But the same account adds that this display of joyful submission to the
"Celestial Khagan" was not quite as simple as it seemed, for the Uighur chief
Tumidu, whom Taizong appointed area commander of Hanhai, "had already
begun calling himself a Khagan in secret and was giving his subordinates
official titles just like those once used by the [Eastern] Türks."[96] It was perhaps
fortunate for Tang interests that Tumidu was assassinated by his nephew *Öghüt
(Wuhe) a year later.

Taizong used his new status as khagan over the eastern Tegreg to establish
a Yanran Protectorate, with a Tang protector-general and deputy protector-
general based in Inner Mongolia to oversee the *jimi* area commands and
prefectures on the steppe.[97] The Protectorate made both its authority and its
ruthlessness known soon after Tumidu's assassination, when it tricked Öghüt
into reporting to Protectorate headquarters to be confirmed as Tumidu's successor. An unsuspecting Öghüt arrived with only a small party of guards and was
immediately arrested and executed. The Tang court than installed Tumidu's son
*Barun (Porun, d. 661) as Hanhai area commander.[98]

A self-assessment that Taizong reportedly delivered to his ministers in 647
has frequently been quoted in modern historical scholarship as embodying early
Tang "cosmopolitanism" in general and Taizong's lack of ethnocentrism in
particular.

> Since antiquity, rulers have pacified the Central Lands of the Chinese but
> have not been able to bring the barbarians to submission. My talent is not
> equal to that of the ancients, yet my success has surpassed theirs .... Since
> antiquity, everyone has seen the Chinese of the Central Lands as superior and
> the barbarians as inferior. I alone love them equally, and that is why their
> tribes have all cleaved to me as if to their own parents.[99]

Taizong's words are certainly appealing to modern liberal sensibilities, as they
appear to ascribe equal worth and dignity to all ethnic groups. But they should
be read in the context of Taizong's penchant for self-promoting, exceptionalist
political rhetoric, and his use of the eastern Tegreg peoples' recent submission
to both neutralize the humiliation of his first Goguryeo invasion and override his
ministers' objections to his plans for a second invasion. The message of
Taizong's rhetoric was that he was uniquely qualified to conquer Goguryeo,

---

[96] *ZZTJ* 198.6244–45.
[97] The protector-general's headquarters was in the area of modern Bayannur, Inner Mongolia. *ZZTJ* 198.6246.
[98] *ZZTJ* 199.6262.   [99] *ZZTJ* 198.6247.

despite his recent failure to do so, because "barbarians" found his affection for them irresistible.[100] With the benefit of historical perspective, we can tell that the real reason for Taizong's successes was the fragility and instability of the Eastern Türk, Western Türk, and Syr-Yanda khaganates and the consequent possibility of using Turkic client cavalry as a potent striking arm in warfare on the Inner Asian frontiers. In other words, it was the weaknesses of Taizong's enemies, not his strengths, that made the real difference. But it served his purposes to promote the idea that Goguryeo would inevitably fall to him because he was simply a singularly enlightened and open-minded ruler.

It did not take Taizong long to begin using his new eastern Tegreg vassals to wage war on more recalcitrant "barbarians," as he had already done with the Kibir and Eastern Türks. In early 648, he mobilized some 100,000 cavalry from the Tegreg and the Eastern Türks for a punitive attack on the Tarim Basin state of Kucha (modern Kuqa, Xinjiang), which was aligned with a faction of the Western Türks.[101] The expedition was jointly commanded by Ashina Zhanir, Kibir Garik, and Anxi protector-general Guo Xiaoke. It first captured the king of Agni (who had, ironically, fled to Kucha to evade the Tang invasion), killed him, and replaced him with a cousin, then overran Kucha relatively quickly in January 649 and captured its king as well. A fierce counterattack by Kuchean loyalists and Western Türks killed Guo Xiaoke and nearly retook the kingdom's capital before being repelled. The Tang expedition then replaced the Kuchean king Haripushpa (Ch. Helibushibi, "Sun Flower" in Sanskrit) with his younger brother and erected a stone inscription to commemorate its victory before returning to Xizhou (Gaochang) with Haripushpa as its prisoner.[102]

Like the Agni expedition of 644, the Kucha expedition had limited aims: not permanent occupation or annexation, but rather removing a ruler seen as hostile to Tang interests and replacing him with someone friendlier to the Tang. In fact, the expedition was ultimately a failure, as the kingdom descended into civil war after the Tang removed Haripushpa. Taizong died in the summer of 649, and his successor Gaozong (Li Zhi, r. 649–83) chose to reinstall Haripushpa as king, returning to the status quo ante bellum. A permanent Tang military presence in the Tarim Basin would not materialize until ten years later, and even this had a rocky start, as we shall see.

---

[100]　See Yang, "What Do Barbarians Know of Gratitude?" 58–60.

[101]　Interestingly, this faction seems to have been led by a rival of the Kül-Chor. Consequently, the Kül-Chor offered to attack Kucha in concert with the Tang expedition. The Tang court does not appear to have accepted this offer. *ZZTJ* 198.6250–51, 199.6259.

[102]　*ZZTJ* 198.6261–65. For a visualization of the campaign with digital maps, see Yang, *Frontiers of the Tang and Song Empires*, Map 1, at https://storymaps.arcgis.com/stories/0cf798878 745406fa5719b97ccfc5454#ref-n-Vqh2gq.

In early 649, Taizong also placed a Tang general in command of Uighur and Buqut cavalry for an attack on *Chabi (Chebi) Khagan, an Eastern Türk leader who had established a khaganate in the Altai Mountains of western Mongolia and defied attempts by both the Syr-Yanda and the Tang to subdue him.[103] This was the last military campaign that Taizong initiated, though he was making preparations for a seaborne invasion of Goguryeo at the time of his death, a massive operation that would have involved 300,000 troops and 1,100 ships – more than double the scale of the 645 invasion.[104] In an unusually honest admission, the *Tang huiyao* notes: "Chabi had committed no crime, but the emperor, having retreated from Anshi (i.e., Goguryeo), wanted to achieve some great feat to wash away his humiliation."[105] In the summer of 650, the Tang expedition captured Chabi and moved his followers to central Mongolia, where they were placed under a new *jimi* area command.[106] The entire Mongolian steppe was now under Tang suzerainty as far west as the Altai. It would remain so for the next thirty-five years.

Chabi Khagan, like several of the Eastern Türk chiefs in 630, was made a commander in the imperial guards after being taken prisoner and brought to Chang'an. Haripushpa briefly received the same treatment before being sent back to Kucha. This was a policy of clemency established by Taizong, who probably believed it would incentivize Inner Asian leaders to surrender peacefully and also demonstrate trust and goodwill to their people. When Chabi was brought before Gaozong, the latter is said to have cited the fact that "the previous emperor always pardoned chieftains whom he had captured" as a reason for pardoning him even though he deserved death for his "crime" of defying the Tang.[107]

Although mainly intended as a tool of diplomacy, the use of defeated Turkic leaders as imperial guard officers also gave the early Tang court a multiethnic and multicultural character. Taizong's first heir apparent Li Chengqian (618–45) apparently became a Turcophile due to the influence of this court environment, as well as the presence of many resettled Türk elite families in Chang'an during his teenage years in the 630s. It should be noted that the Yang and Li imperial families of Sui and Tang had intermarried with prominent families of Inner Asian Serbi (Xianbei) origin in the late sixth and early seventh centuries, as Serbi dynasties had ruled in north China for nearly two centuries before the founding of the Sui. Taizong's empress, Chengqian's mother, was herself from the Serbi Zhangsun clan, and Taizong's mother was from another Serbi clan, the

---

[103] An earlier attempt by a Tang embassy to kidnap Chabi had ended in the death of both envoys. *ZZTJ* 198.6250, 199.6265–66.

[104] Taizong had been trying to persuade his ministers to agree to a second Goguryeo invasion since 646. A massive shipbuilding project was started in Sichuan in 648 and soon caused significant discontent and hardship there. Taizong's ministers were perhaps secretly relieved that he died in 649 before his new obsession with Goguryeo made him a second Yangdi.

[105] *THY* 94.1690.   [106] *ZZTJ* 199.6271–72.   [107] *XTS* 215a.6042; *CFYG* 986.11409.

Dou. But the elite Serbi clans of north China had abandoned their steppe customs and acculturated to Sinitic mores by the early seventh century, to the extent of viewing other steppe peoples as barbarians and losing much of their command of the Serbi language.[108] It is misleading, therefore, to interpret Li Chengqian's Turcophilia as a manifestation of the Tang imperial family's Inner Asian heritage rather than a result of his contact with elite Türks who would have appeared intriguingly exotic in the milieu of Chang'an high society.[109]

According to his official biography, Li Chengqian spoke fluent Turkic and enjoyed roleplaying as a Türk khagan: dressed in steppe-style clothes and braided pigtails, dining on mutton in a tent with attendants picked for their Türk-like or Sogdian-like facial features. He reportedly also once acted out a khagan's funeral, with attendants riding horses around his "body" and slashing their faces with knives in accordance with Turkic mourning custom.[110] One can hardly fault Li Chengqian for this sort of cultural appropriation, given his own father's embrace of the Celestial Khagan persona – in fact, Turkic envoys and imperial guard officers in Chang'an are said to have mourned Taizong's death by mutilating their faces and ears and cutting their pigtails off.[111] But Chengqian's taste for Turkic folkways gave rise to scurrilous rumors, probably spread by his bookish brother and rival Li Tai (620–53), that he had expressed a wish to "become a Türk" and hand the empire over to Ashina Simurgh as soon as he succeeded Taizong as emperor. As a result of these rumors and other (similarly dubious) accusations that charged him with plotting to assassinate both Li Tai and Taizong, Chengqian was deposed, stripped of royal status, and placed under house arrest in 643, dying in exile two years later. Unfortunately for Li Tai, he had overreached in the process of destroying Chengqian and exposed his unscrupulous ambition for the throne. He, too, was soon sent into exile and the position of heir apparent went to his unassuming younger brother Li Zhi, the future Gaozong.[112]

4 Expansion in Central Asia and Korea (650–670)

Modern accounts of Chinese history tend to give Gaozong's reign short shrift compared to Taizong's: It is Taizong, not Gaozong, who is often lionized as China's greatest emperor and empire-builder. This is unfair, since Gaozong

---

[108] Holcombe, "The Xianbei"; Holcombe, "Chinese Identity."

[109] On this, I disagree with the interpretation of the early Tang emperors as ethnoculturally more Inner Asian (or Turkic) than Chinese, proposed by Sanping Chen and a number of Japanese Sinologists including Sugiyama Masaaki and Moriyasu Takao. Chen, *Multicultural China*; Moriyasu, *Shirukurōdo*.

[110] *XTS* 80.3564–65; *ZZTJ* 196.6189–90.

[111] Ashina Zhanir and Kibir Garik supposedly even volunteered to commit suicide and be buried with Taizong, but Gaozong vetoed their requests. *ZZTJ* 199.6268–69.

[112] *ZZTJ* 196.6190–92, 197.6193–97; *XTS* 80.3564–65.

(unlike Taizong) succeeded in expanding the Tang empire into the Tarim Basin, Liaodong, and Korea, whereas the only territorial gains made by Taizong were relatively minor: Yiwu, Gaochang, and Beshbalik. Part of the problem stems from a misconception that Taizong *did* conquer the Tarim Basin when he briefly took Kucha in 648. There's also the issue of conflating symbolic expansion via the creation of *jimi* polities with actual military occupation: It's often thought that Taizong "conquered" the entire Mongolian steppe by incorporating it into the *jimi* system in 647, though this was only a form of suzerainty and not a conquest *stricto sensu*. But even by that measure, Gaozong at least equaled Taizong's record by extending the *jimi* system as far west as Uzbekistan and Afghanistan.

Perhaps the key difference, then, is that Taizong benefited greatly from later Tang historians' tendency to idealize him as a model Confucian ruler, though they (unlike modern historians) typically downplayed his wars of conquest or exaggerated his willingness to eschew expansionism.[113] Gaozong's legacy, in contrast, was marred by these same historians' misogynistic perceptions of him as weak-willed and dominated by the highly intelligent but ruthless Empress Wu, who supposedly was the real power behind the throne.[114] Gaozong was unfairly condemned for sharing power with his wife and treating her as an equal partner – something anathema to patriarchal Confucians, though we might actually see it as enlightened today.[115]

Though Gaozong lacked Taizong's experience as a military commander, he was not necessarily much less able, energetic, or effective as a ruler. It's true that after 660, he was periodically incapacitated by vertigo and during those situations allowed Empress Wu to make policy decisions on his behalf in a kind of co-rulership arrangement. In 675, he even considered appointing Empress Wu as regent, but was dissuaded by a minister who insisted that an empress had no place holding political power.[116] But Gaozong was still in full control in 656–60, the period of the empire's wars of expansion into Central Asia and Baekje, and he is not known to have delegated decision-making over those wars to his empress or anyone else. Although the empire was forced to retreat from both Central Asia and Korea later in his reign, neither his physical decline nor

---

[113] For a translation of the early eighth-century text that was pivotal in constructing an idealized image of Taizong, see Wu, *The Essentials of Governance*. Interestingly, its author depicted Taizong as following his ministers' advice to avoid wars of expansion, rather than as an avid expansionist.

[114] For example, *ZZTJ* 201.6342–43.   [115] Rothschild, *Wu Zhao*, 49–51.

[116] *JTS* 6.115; *ZZTJ* 200.6322, 202.6375–76. Many modern historians assume that Gaozong's vertigo was a complication from a stroke or series of strokes, but the ailment began when he was thirty-two – an age at which strokes are possible but far from common. More circumspection as to its causes seems advisable.

Empress Wu's involvement in politics can be blamed for this. Instead, the Tang conquests in both Taizong's and Gaozong's reigns were simply overly dependent on the use of Turkic cavalry, the use of allies to undermine an opponent's defensive strengths, and a geopolitical situation that allowed Tang armies to take the offensive without worrying much about frontier defense. Once circumstances changed and these options were no longer available, the Tang was forced to pull back and adopt a more cautious grand strategy.

Gaozong's first major foreign policy challenge came from Ashina *Garo (Helu), a Western Türk chief who had submitted to Taizong in 648 and received appointment as a *jimi* area commander in the Dzungarian Basin. In 650, Garo led his followers deep into Central Asia, defeated Ibil Sheguy Khagan, and unified the Western Türk tribes, adopting the title Ishbara (Shaboluo) Khagan. He soon began raids aimed at pushing the Tang out of Beshbalik. In 655, Gaozong made an attempt at undermining Ishbara by recognizing one of his rivals as khagan, but Ishbara's army blocked Gaozong's envoy from delivering an edict of investiture to the challenger. Gaozong then decided on military action to destroy Ishbara's khaganate. In 656–7, the Yanran Protectorate mobilized the Uighurs and Buqut for an attack on the Western Türks across the Altai Mountains.[117] This was challenging and unfamiliar terrain that Chinese armies would normally have had immense difficulty navigating, but the Tegreg contingent guided a Tang expeditionary force under general Su Dingfang (d. 667) all the way to the banks of the upper Irtysh River (the Kara-Irtysh). There, the combined Tegreg–Tang army routed Ishbara's forces. Ishbara fled and sought sanctuary in the Sogdian state of Chach (Tashkent) but was betrayed and handed over to pursuing Tegreg forces led by the Yanran deputy protector-general.

Gaozong divided the Western Türk heartland, between the Ili and Syr Darya river basins, into two client khaganates, each under a Western Türk chief who had defected to the Tang in 639–40. Each khaganate had authority over five of the ten core Western Türk tribes and was officially designated as a protectorate, with its khagan as the protector-general – essentially a variation on the *jimi* system. The campaign's focus then shifted to the Western Türks' former sphere of influence in the Tarim Basin. In 658, a Tang army crushed a pro-Türk revolt at Kucha and massacred its leaders, upon which the headquarters of the Anxi Protectorate moved to Kucha from Xizhou (Gaochang). City-states in the western and southwestern areas of the Tarim Basin, including Shulik (Shule) and Khotan, continued to resist the Tang in alliance with Western Türk holdouts

---

[117] Official Tang sources record the participation of the Uighurs, while the Chinese epitaph of the Buqut chief *Itü (Yitu, 635–78), discovered in central Mongolia in 2009, shows that the Buqut were involved as well. The Chinese text of the epitaph can be found here: https://en.wikipedia.org/wiki/Epitaph_of_Pugu_Yitu#Inscription.

until late 659 or early 660, when they surrendered to Su Dingfang. It was presumably in 660, therefore, that the Tang first established the so-called Four Garrisons of Anxi in Agni, Kucha, Khotan, and Shulik. This was not outright annexation: The kings of these states retained their positions, holding area commander posts in the *jimi* system. But unlike the leaders of most *jimi* polities, including the Western Türk protectorates, they were now compelled to host Tang military forces on their territory to ensure they would not align with other powers. This was a form of power projection and military hegemony similar to modern overseas military bases. The sources give no indication of the size of these garrisons, but subsequent events suggest they were relatively weak, being intended to suppress local revolts only.

It is often claimed that Tang conquest of the Tarim Basin "reopened" the Silk Road or at least made it safer for traveling merchants. This is a misconception based partly on a Chinese stereotype of steppe nomads like the Western Türks as rapacious and violent raiders, when in fact the Türks relied heavily on both trading and tributary relations with the Central Asian city-states for resources that were scarce on the steppe.[118] It was in their interest to keep the caravan routes safe from bandits, though the civil wars among the Western Türks, which occasionally involved attacks on Sogdian states, probably did disrupt trade to some extent. That being said, it is not self-evident that Tang domination in Central Asia would have made things any better for the silk trade: The Tang state's *Statutes on Custom Barriers and Marketplaces* (*Guanshi ling*) prohibited exporting most forms of silk textile, as well as gold, silver, iron, hemp linen, pearls and yak tails (popular for adorning standards, banners, and carriages), to countries beyond the empire's western and northern frontiers.[119] This list of embargoed goods already existed in 652 and apparently remained in force throughout Tang history, with occasional modifications: updated lists are known from 714, 737, and 780, and the 780 list (which apparently banned the export of slaves for the first time) was still current law as of 836, by which time it evidently also was applied to maritime trade.[120] In fact, the 737 statutes also banned Tang subjects from bringing the finest weaves of silk to the Lingnan region (Guangdong and Guangxi), presumably to prevent these high-value commodities from being exported by sea through the port of Guangzhou (Canton).

The range of Chinese goods available to foreigners through legal private trade would therefore not have included the luxury products in greatest demand among Inner Asians, such as silk. In fact, Tang law did not allow ordinary imperial subjects to leave the country to engage in trade at all. Persons caught

---

[118] Iwami, "Turks and Sogdians," 48–49.   [119] *TLSY* 8.176–77.
[120] *THY* 86.1581; Kao ed., *Tiansheng ling yizhu*, 343–45; *CFYG* 99.11562–63.

crossing the frontier to trade with "foreigners" (*huawairen*) would be punished with at least two years of penal servitude, with the severity of punishment increasing according to the value of goods traded. If the value came up to fifteen or more bolts of silk, then the penalty was both life exile and three years of penal servitude.[121] Only expatriate Sogdian merchants registered as permanent residents in the empire's westernmost regular prefectures, the so-called "*Hu* merchants" (*xingsheng Hu* or *xinghu*), were normally allowed to travel to foreign countries for commerce, provided they paid taxes through their prefecture of registration.[122]

The main purpose of both the ban on foreign trade by Chinese merchants and the embargo on export of valuable prestige goods by Sogdian expatriate merchants was probably to prevent foreign rulers from gaining access to such goods without paying tribute to the emperor. Unrestricted export by private merchants would have undermined both the court's ability to amass them for use as diplomatic gifts, and foreign rulers' motivation to present tribute in exchange for such gifts. Of course, there probably *was* private foreign trade in silk and other embargoed goods along the Tang frontiers in Central Asia, but any such trade was effectively smuggling, carried out in violation of imperial law. This fact is almost never acknowledged in modern studies of the Silk Road, which tend to emphasize the Tang government's role in protecting and promoting international trade. It has recently been argued that long-distance silk trade in Central Asia only flourished when Tang military forces were stationed in the Tarim Basin, since the troops were typically paid with bolts of silk, which they then traded for daily necessities.[123] I would refine this theory further by suggesting that while long-distance silk trade may have increased *within* the Tarim Basin because of the Tang military presence, that same presence was meant to prevent Chinese silk from moving further west (e.g., into Sogdiana), except through the tributary system.

Gaozong also sought to extend his sway over other Central Asian polities that had been subject to Western Türk suzerainty. Between 658 and 661, he sent envoys to confer *jimi* area commander titles to the rulers of various states in Sogdiana and Tokharistan. The envoys were also instructed to collect information on the customs, products, and histories of each state and to map its geographical features. Their ethnographic reports and maps were compiled into an *Illustrated Gazetteer of the Western Regions*, unfortunately now lost.[124] Any ruler who

---

[121] Tang ambassadors were also forbidden to trade privately when abroad, but this rule was apparently broken on a regular basis because of the handsome profits to be made. *TLSY* 8.177–78; *JTS* 138.2567, 149.2729.

[122] Arakawa, "Aspects of Sogdian Trading Activities," 30–32.

[123] Hansen, *The Silk Road*, 169–70, 175.   [124] *ZZTJ* 200.6324–25; *THY* 73.1323–25.

accepted a nominal post as area commander was technically answerable to the Anxi protector-general at Kucha, who really had almost no way of controlling them across such a great distance. Prefectures, counties, and military units were created for each area command, all of them under members of the local elite and only nominally subject to Tang jurisdiction.[125]

The extension of Chinese imperial influence into western Central Asia was an exercise in stretching the *jimi* system to unrealistic extremes. This is evident from the case of the "area command" of Bosi ("Persia"), the "area commander" of which was Piruz (Ch. Beilusi), a son of Yazdegerd III (r. 632–51), the last Shahanshah (King of Kings) of Sassanian Iran. The rising Arabo-Islamic empire had invaded the Sassanian empire in the 630s and 640s, conquering first Iraq and then Iran and driving Yazdegerd east to Merv in the Khorasan region, where he was murdered by a local lord in 651. By 654, according to Tang records, Piruz had taken refuge from the Arab armies in the mountains of Tokharistan (Bactria), where he received support from local Turkic rulers. In 661, he sent an envoy to the Tang court requesting military aid in regaining his father's empire. Gaozong responded by creating a "Bosi area command" at Piruz's base of operations in Zaranj, near Afghanistan's modern border with Iran. The Tang further awarded Piruz the title "King of Bosi" in early 662.[126] Piruz's formal status as Gaozong's vassal has served as the basis for claims that the Tang empire at its height extended as far as the eastern borders of Iran. But no Tang army was deployed to Sogdiana or Tokharistan at this time, and there was not even a discussion at the Tang court about whether to go to war with the Arabs on behalf of the "King of Bosi."[127] This is not surprising, since Gaozong's attention had shifted to the Korean peninsula by then.

In the fall of 660, ships carrying some 100,000 Tang troops crossed the Yellow Sea from the Shandong peninsula and sailed to the western coast of today's South Korea. There, they fought their way up the Geum River to attack Sabi (modern Buyeo County, South Chungcheong province), the capital of the Baekje kingdom (Figure 5). Simultaneously, the army of Silla attacked by land from the east, pinning down a part of Baekje's military. Su Dingfang, fresh from his victories in Central Asia, commanded the Tang invasion force. He routed a Baekje army outside Sabi, besieged the city, and soon received the surrender of Baekje's royal family.

---

[125] According to Tang records, 16 area commands, 70 to 80 prefectures, 110 counties, and 126 military units were created in Tokharistan alone. A commemorative stele was erected in Tokharistan with an inscription listing all their names, but no remains of it have been found.

[126] Wang, *Tang, Tufan, Dashi*, 92–95.

[127] See Yang, *Frontiers of the Tang and Song Empires*, Map 3 and Map 4, at https://storymaps .arcgis.com/stories/0cf798878745406fa5719b97ccfc5454#ref-n-CgqSVa and https://storymaps .arcgis.com/stories/0cf798878745406fa5719b97ccfc5454#ref-n-NERPth.

Figure 5 Map of Goguryeo, Baekje, and Silla at the time of the Tang invasions, with capital cities marked by red stars. (Source: Wikimedia Commons)

This joint operation was the fruit of repeated appeals that Silla had made to the Tang since the 640s for military aid against Goguryeo and Baekje, who had formed an alliance aimed at retaking territory lost to Silla's expansion since the mid-sixth century.[128] The Tang, for its part, recognized an opportunity to strike at Goguryeo from the south by moving armies through Baekje and Silla, thus bypassing the Liaodong defensive system that had defeated Yangdi and Taizong alike, while also avoiding the greater risks of directly attacking Pyongyang by sea. Gaozong's recent successes in Central Asia appear to have inspired him to prove himself his father's equal by solving the seemingly intractable Goguryeo problem.

The Tang court quickly incorporated the former Baekje into its administrative system, appointing local leaders as area commanders and prefects. This was not a true *jimi* arrangement and more like a military occupation, since the Baekje king was sent into captivity in Chang'an and no new monarch was installed. Su Dingfang left a small force behind to protect his rear while taking most of his army north to attack Goguryeo in early 661. In coordination with Su, a combined Tang–Uighur army opened up a second front against Goguryeo in Liaodong. Evidently thrilled by his string of successes in Central Asia and Korea, Gaozong made plans to emulate Taizong by traveling to Liaodong to command the Goguryeo invasion in person. He was dissuaded by Empress Wu, probably on the grounds that the hardships of military campaigning would further jeopardize his health.[129]

---

[128] *ZZTJ* 197.6204, 199.6261, 6287, 200.6320.   [129] *ZZTJ* 200.6322–24.

At this point, things began to go awry for the Tang on multiple fronts and frontiers. Before marching on Goguryeo, Su Dingfang had permitted his troops to plunder Baekje and apparently also carried out massacres of able-bodied Baekje men, presumably to preempt rebellion.[130] This cruel strategy backfired as anti-Tang revolts soon broke out, forcing the occupation force to call for reinforcements from both China and Silla. Japan, a long-time ally of Baekje, then entered the conflict: It was holding a Baekje prince as a diplomatic hostage and now returned him to his country to assume leadership over the growing insurgency, with support from a large Japanese expeditionary force.[131]

While his colleagues struggled to regain control in Baekje, Su Dingfang defeated Goguryeo's armies and began besieging Pyongyang. But the invasion's Liaodong prong had to be aborted when the Uighur chief Barun suddenly died and his successor broke with the Tang, joining a coalition of Tegreg peoples that had revolted against Tang domination in 660.[132] Pyongyang held out successfully, and Su Dingfang had to withdraw to Silla when a snowstorm endangered his supply lines. The Tang occupation force in Baekje did manage to defeat the insurgents and their Japanese allies in 663, with significant assistance from the army of Silla, but it was a hollow victory that left Baekje's cities gutted and littered with the dead.[133] Nevertheless, Japan's failed intervention in Baekje, which cost it some 400 ships' worth of soldiers, decisively ended its history of military involvement on the East Asian mainland for over nine centuries. Fear of a Chinese punitive invasion is also believed to have given impetus, at least for several decades, to the Japanese state's efforts at building centralized political, legal, and military systems modeled on those of the Tang.[134] By using Baekje's fate as a warning, the state could override local chiefly elites' reluctance to surrender their powers under a new model of provincial administration.

In 662, shortly after Su Dingfang's retreat from Pyongyang, the rebel Tegreg coalition surrendered to a Tang punitive expedition. Tang forces executed more than 200 chiefs and nobles in reprisal for their role in the revolt.[135] Early the next year, the headquarters of the Yanran Protectorate moved from Inner Mongolia to the Uighur homeland in central Mongolia and was renamed the

---

[130] *ZZTJ* 201.6337. On the use of such massacres in Tang warfare, see Yang, "Letting the Troops Loose."

[131] *ZZTJ* 200.6323–24.

[132] The cause of the revolt is unknown, but it may have to do with dissatisfaction over having to do so much campaigning for the Tang empire in recent years. *ZZTJ* 200.6322, 6325–26.

[133] *ZZTJ* 200.6327, 6329–30, 201.6336–38.

[134] Batten, "Foreign Threat and Domestic Reform."

[135] *ZZTJ* 200.6327–29. One source (*THY* 68.1068) claims that the expedition massacred over 100,000 Tegreg, but I have argued elsewhere that this is a misreading of an earlier account of a much smaller massacre (itself likely fabricated): Yang, "Letting the Troops Loose," 23–27.

Hanhai Protectorate; it was again renamed the Anbei (Pacifying the North) Protectorate in 669. This established a Tang military presence on the steppe for the first time, in the form of a garrisoned fort, for the purpose of monitoring Tegreg activities and preempting further revolts.[136] However, the Tang military would not be able to mobilize the Tegreg as cavalry for new campaigns until the steppe situation stabilized. The sole exceptions were the Kibir, whose leader Garik had become one of the Tang's best generals and played a key role in persuading the Tegreg rebels to surrender.[137]

Meanwhile, all was not quiet on the western front, as the Tibetan empire began attacking the Tuygun khaganate and the Tang garrison at Shulik in 660–2.[138] Many historians have interpreted the Tibetans as opportunistic expansionists pursuing control over the prime horse pastures of Qinghai and the trade routes through the Tarim Basin. We do not have Tibetan sources from this period to give their side of the story. But given that the Tibetans had avoided conflict with the Tang for the preceding two decades, it is also possible that the new Tang military presence in Central Asia led them to fear being attacked from both the north and northeast at once. If so, then their actions were defensive and preemptive, aimed at removing Tang forces and pro-Tang regimes from their frontiers and creating buffer zones.

In 663, Tibetan attacks routed the Tuygun and drove khagan Nagaput, Princess Honghua, and their pro-Tang faction into exile in Tang-controlled Gansu. Gaozong had earlier refused to intervene in the Tibetan–Tuygun conflict, opting for a posture of impartiality; now it was too late. The Tibetans installed a client khagan of their own and stationed a large army in the Tuygun lands to guard against Tang intervention and project power into the lands of the Qiang and Tanguts. In the Tarim Basin, the Tibetans found local allies in the Western Türk *Köngül (Gongyue) tribe and the state of Shulik, which had apparently eliminated its Tang garrison with Tibetan help. The Tibetan–Köngül–Shulik alliance began attacking Khotan by 665. The Tang response to these incursions was hampered not only by the temporary unavailability of the eastern Tegreg but also by the Anxi Protectorate's mishandling of a bitter rivalry between the two Western Türk client khagans. The protector-general summarily executed one of the khagans on trumped-up charges of treason made by the other, which alienated more of the Western Türk tribes and led them to transfer their support to the Tibetans.[139]

---

[136] Sources on the history of the Yanran and Hanhai protectorates are confusingly contradictory, resulting in different interpretations. My narrative here follows a recent study by Li Danjie. *ZZTJ* 201.6333; Li, "Hanhai duhu fu."
[137] *ZZTJ* 200.6325–26, 6328–29.　　[138] *ZZTJ* 200.6321, 201.6332–33.
[139] *ZZTJ* 201.6332–33, 6334–36, 6339, 6344.

With the benefit of hindsight, one can see that the Tang had neglected to consolidate its expansion into Central Asia properly before turning to Korea, and that it had been complacent in underestimating the Tibetans and taking its Tegreg vassals for granted. But as of 665–6, Gaozong was still in a relatively triumphant mood. That winter, he led a grand procession from Luoyang to Mount Tai in Shandong, where on the day of the Lunar New Year he became the first Tang emperor to perform the prestigious Feng and Shan sacrifices to Heaven and Earth, symbolically announcing to the world that he had achieved an age of great peace and prosperity.[140] Those present included envoys from the Central Asian states, the Eastern and Western Türks, the Tegreg, occupied Baekje, Silla, Japan, and even Goguryeo, all summoned to witness Gaozong's moment of glory.[141]

If the leaders of Goguryeo hoped that flattering Gaozong's ego at Mount Tai would head off another war, those hopes soon proved unfounded when he announced a new campaign against Pyongyang in the summer of 666. Yeon Gaesomun had recently died, and conflict had broken out among his three sons. Facing defeat by his brothers, the eldest son Namsaeng (634–79) defected to the Tang and provided information crucial to breaking through his kingdom's defenses in Liaodong. In 667–8, the combined armies of the Tang and Yeon Namsaeng overran the Liaodong fortresses, crossed the Yalu River, and joined forces with a Silla army to besiege and capture Pyongyang. In the end, the Baekje campaign turned out to be a costly sideshow: disunity among Goguryeo's rulers was enough to destroy their kingdom without any involvement by Tang forces in Baekje. Gaozong established an Andong (Pacifying the East) Protectorate at Pyongyang, with a garrison of 20,000 troops, and effectively annexed Goguryeo, dividing it into area commands, prefectures, and counties led by local elites who were regarded as reliable collaborators. To avoid a repeat of the revolt in Baekje, Chinese officials were brought in to "co-administer" these area commands, and about 4–6 percent of the population was forcibly resettled in China – this probably included most of the aristocracy, as one source claims that only "the poor and weak" were left behind.[142]

5 A Concatenation of Frontier Crises (670–700)

In late 669 Gaozong's court, flushed with success after the long-sought conquest of Goguryeo, began discussing whether to launch an attack on the Tibetans to regain control over the Tuygun khaganate. The debate was deadlocked due to

---

[140] Taizong had planned to perform the Feng and Shan in 642 but cancelled them due to an inauspicious astrological omen. Another plan to perform the Feng and Shan was cancelled in 647 due to floods in Hebei. *ZZTJ* 196.6165, 6168, 198.6242, 6245, 6248.

[141] *ZZTJ* 201.6344–46.

[142] The *Tongdian* gives the number of resettled households as 28,200, but the *Zizhi tongjian* has 38,200. *TD* 186.5019; *ZZTJ* 201.6356–57, 6359.

concerns over the effects of drought and famine in both north and south China during the previous year.[143] By then, both Shulik and Khotan had become Tibetan allies, so the Four Garrisons were down to two. The Tang court was finally forced to act in the summer of 670 when Tibetan and Khotanese forces captured the city of Baruka (Bohuan, modern Aksu), posing a direct threat to Kucha to its east. Rather than try and hold the line in the Tarim Basin, the Tang court decided to evacuate the Kucha and Agni garrisons to Xizhou, while sending an army of over 100,000 into the Tuygun lands to expel the Tibetan army there. This expedition ended in disaster for the Tang despite being commanded by Xue Rengui (614–83), a general who had been unbeaten against Goguryeo just two years before. Near Lake Qinghai (Kokonor), a Tibetan army said to have numbered 200,000 intercepted and captured the Tang expedition's supply train. Xue Rengui's army was then trapped and annihilated, reportedly by another 400,000 Tibetan troops. The Tibetans took Xue and his two deputy commanders alive but released them after extracting an informal "peace agreement."[144]

This shocking defeat, together with the preceding collapse of Tang imperial interests in Central Asia, can be attributed to superior strategy on the Tibetan side and overconfidence on the Tang side. But it also highlighted how profoundly the first (and only) imperial power to emerge from the heart of the Tibetan plateau had changed the balance of geopolitics of eastern Eurasia, just as the Arabo-Islamic empire's rise had changed the balance in Eurasia's western half.[145] The Han empire had easily overpowered the unstable coalitions of Qiang tribes in eastern Qinghai, though revolts by resettled Qiang tribes did wreak havoc on Gansu and Shaanxi in the first and second centuries CE. The politically decentralized Tuygun khaganate had likewise been no match for the Sui and Tang military machines, especially when those were supported by Turkic cavalry forces.[146] The Tibetan empire was a completely new factor in Eurasian history: an Inner Asian empire that was both shielded from invasion by geography, and capable of taxing and conscripting its population in order to

---

[143] *ZZTJ* 201.6357, 6359; *CFYG* 991.11479.

[144] One of the deputies was Ashina Zhanir's son Daozhen, which suggests that a continent of Eastern Türks fought in the campaign. Daozhen proved less talented than his father and was demoted to the status of a commoner after this defeat. *ZZTJ* 201.6363–64; *XTS* 110.4116, 111.4142, 216a.6076.

[145] For a visualization of the Arabo-Islamic and Tibetan conquests, see Yang, *Frontiers of the Tang and Song Empires*, Map 4, at https://storymaps.arcgis.com/stories/0cf798878745406 fa5719b97ccfc5454#ref-n-NERPth.

[146] In 608, Pei Shiju persuaded some western Tegreg groups to attack the Tuygun to weaken them in advance of the Sui invasion: *ZZTJ* 181.5641. As we have seen, the Tang invasion of the Tuygun in 634–5 also included Kibir and Eastern Türk cavalry.

field well-trained, well-armored, and highly motivated troops in the hundreds of thousands.[147]

Soon after the Tang defeat in Qinghai, the situation in the Andong Protectorate deteriorated rapidly. Goguryeo loyalists rebelled against the Tang occupation and, by late 671, were receiving military support from Silla. Silla's king Munmu (Kim Beopmin, r. 661–81) had played a key role in the suppression of the earlier Baekje revolt and had been "rewarded" with a *jimi* area command in 663. He had also contributed to the Tang conquest of Goguryeo in 668. What, then, explains his sudden abandonment of the military alliance that his predecessors had long sought? Apparently, Munmu had become frustrated with Tang attempts at restraining him from making war on the former Baekje, which was now effectively a Tang satellite state under the nominal authority of a Baekje prince appointed as an area commander. Although Tang troops had pulled out of Baekje in 665, border clashes between Baekje and Silla (which Munmu claimed were provoked by Baekje's aggression) led to their return in 671. That summer, a combined Tang–Baekje force fought a raiding Silla army and suffered defeat. A month later, the Tang demanded that Munmu explain his act of "rebellion." He responded by claiming to have been maligned by Baekje, but also accused the Tang of abandoning a faithful ally to side with a former enemy and of breaking a promise, supposedly made by Taizong in 648, to hand Baekje over to Silla after conquering it. That winter, Munmu began sending troops into Andong to aid the Goguryeo rebels, while providing safe haven to insurgents evading capture by the Tang.[148]

By 674, Munmu had driven the Tang army out of Baekje and annexed it to his kingdom. Gaozong, enraged by this setback, unilaterally "deposed" Munmu and appointed his younger brother Kim Inmun (629–94), who had recently arrived at the Tang court as an ambassador, to replace him. After numerous battles with Tang armies based in Pyongyang, Munmu shifted to a diplomatic strategy and sent a tribute mission to Chang'an conveying apologies for his actions. Gaozong promptly "pardoned" Munmu, "reinstated" him as king, and used this as an opening to give up Pyongyang rather than get sucked into

---

[147] On the Tibetan empire's taxation and conscription systems, see Dotson, *The Old Tibetan Annals*, 47–56. The *Xin Tangshu* (*XTS* 216a.6073) describes the Tibetan military as follows: "Their armor and helmets are of very fine quality, covering the entire body except for two eyeholes. Even strong bows and sharp blades cannot wound them greatly. Their military discipline is strict, but their armies have no food supplies and simply live off plunder. In battle, the units in the rear do not move in until every soldier in the front units has been killed." If this description is accurate, the Tibetan army was designed for both high survivability in battle and strong motivation toward achieving victory.

[148] Kim, *Samguk sagi*, 6.127–28, 7.145–50.

a quagmire in Korea.[149] In 676, the Andong Protectorate was relocated to Liaodong, the Chinese officials sent to "co-administer" Goguryeo were reassigned, and Tang military forces left the Korean peninsula, never to return. It was an ignominious end to an irredentist obsession that had consumed East Asian geopolitics since the Sui reunification of 589.

Gaozong soon attempted to restore the kingdoms of Goguryeo and Baekje as satellite principalities in Liaodong, but this quickly failed as the rulers installed proved unreliable. Most of the captive Koreans used to settle these colonies eventually absconded northwards to join the *Margat (Mohe/Malgal), a collection of Tungusic-speaking chiefdoms in Manchuria who had formerly been vassals of Goguryeo.[150] Meanwhile, Silla stopped its northward expansion just south of Pyongyang and never occupied the city, probably to avoid giving the Tang a pretext for war. This allowed the Tang to continue claiming that its Andong Protectorate extended as far as Pyongyang, a face-saving fiction still reflected in some modern Chinese maps depicting Tang borders in the eighth century. In reality, the area between the Yalu and Taedong rivers remained a stateless buffer zone until the early tenth century, when it came under the rule of the Goryeo (Koryŏ) kingdom.[151] Silla's choice not to threaten Pyongyang soon paid off: Gaozong reportedly contemplated a punitive attack on Silla in 678 but was dissuaded on the grounds that since the empire could not afford to wage war on two fronts, it should prioritize the more dangerous Tibetans, who had begun raiding Tang prefectures adjacent to Qinghai after Gaozong rejected their peace terms in 676. By this time, Gaozong had assembled a punitive expedition of 180,000 troops and sent it into the Tuygun lands. This army suffered another ignominious defeat on the shores of Lake Qinghai, due mainly to the military inexperience of the civilian minister tasked with overall command.[152]

After this second debacle in Qinghai, Gaozong's ministers were divided over the best strategy for dealing with Tibet: attack again, strengthen frontier defenses, or sue for peace?[153] In the end, the defensive approach won out under the only Tang commander to distinguish himself in the second Qinghai campaign: Heukchi Sangji (Ch. Heichi Changzhi, 630–89), whose daring night raid on the Tibetan camp helped part of the Tang force to retreat safely. Sangji

---

[149] Kim Inmun was then already en route to Silla, but Gaozong recalled him to Chang'an and rescinded his appointment as king. Inmun spent nineteen more years in Chang'an, effectively serving as a diplomatic hostage, and died there in 694. *ZZTJ* 202.6372, 6374.

[150] *ZZTJ* 202.6378–79, 6382–83. My use of *Margat* as the original form of the ethnonym follows Christopher Atwood. The Sinographic transcription of the ethnonym is read as Mohe in modern Mandarin and Malgal in modern Korean. It would have been *Matgat* in the Middle Chinese of Tang times.

[151] Kim, "A Buffer Zone for Peace."   [152] *ZZTJ* 202.6375, 6379–80, 6383–86.

[153] *ZZTJ* 202.6386; *CFYG* 991.11479–80.

was a former officer in the Baekje army who had been recruited into the Tang military in the 660s, despite having earlier participated in the anti-Tang revolt in Baekje. By 680, he held overall command on the Qinghai front and began strengthening its defenses significantly with a system of watchtowers and agricultural colonies, which is said to have eventually deterred the Tibetans from raiding. Sangji was one of the most effective Tang generals of the 680s but was falsely accused of treason in 689 and committed suicide while in prison awaiting trial.[154] His career, like those of Kibir Garik and Ashina Zhanir, illustrates the viability of military talent as a path to social mobility for ethnically non-Chinese subjects of the Tang empire, including members of conquered peoples. But it also reflects how such "foreign" military men, lacking strong social connections at the imperial court, could be vulnerable to slander by their enemies and were heavily dependent on the emperor's trust and favor.[155]

Although the Tibetans did not deploy permanent military garrisons to the Tarim Basin, they were capable of sending in strong expeditionary armies if necessary. The Tang court, seeing Qinghai as the more critical front, thus opted not to mount an offensive in Central Asia and contented itself with nominal displays of submission by the Köngül, Shulik, and Khotan in 674–5.[156] The ten tribes of the Western Türks, now under the leadership of the khagan Ashina *Tochi (Duzhi), had broken with the Tang and realigned themselves with the Tibetans, but the Tang similarly lacked the wherewithal to mount a punitive expedition against them while the Qinghai front remained insecure. This was the background to the most bizarre military operation in Tang history. In 674, the "Bosi area commander" Piruz and his son Narseh (Ch. Ninieshi) had traveled from Tokharistan to the Tang court, perhaps to make a personal appeal for military action against the Arabs (who had begun raiding Sogdiana from Khorasan). Piruz later died in Chang'an, and Gaozong detained Narseh as a hostage rather than let him return to Tokharistan and take his father's place. In 679, general Pei Xingjian (619–82) persuaded Gaozong to let him lead

---

[154] *JTS* 109.3294–95; *XTS* 110.4121–22; *ZZTJ* 201.6337–68, 202.6386, 6395, 6401, 204.6461.

[155] See Yang, *Late Tang China and the World*, Section 3, for a more infamous case of this problem, the rebellion of the Turco-Sogdian general An Lushan.

[156] *ZZTJ* 202.6371–72, 6374–75. Because the ruler of each state or tribe visited the Tang court during these years to offer his surrender, some Japanese and Chinese historians have seen this as evidence that the Tang recaptured the Tarim Basin by 675, only to lose it again to the Western Türks and Tibetans in 678. I find it more likely that these visits to Chang'an were a form of diplomatic maneuvering to forestall a Tang counterattack. The sole extant source on them states that the Köngül and Shulik rulers came to Chang'an in early 674 after hearing that Gaozong was about to launch a punitive expedition against them. Gaozong "pardoned" them, sent them back to their states, and apparently called off the attack. Wang Xiaofu has argued that the attack did proceed and succeeded in retaking the Four Garrisons, but I find his evidence unpersuasive. Christopher Beckwith has an alternative interpretation of these rulers as deposed exiles, which I likewise find unlikely. Beckwith, *The Tibetan Empire*, 199–200; Wang, *Tang, Tufan, Dashi*, 73–75.

a mission through the Western Türk lands, ostensibly to escort Narseh back to his "kingdom" but in reality to lure Ashina Tochi into a trap. The unsuspecting Tochi accepted an invitation to a hunting expedition and was arrested upon showing up. Narseh's military "escort" then left him to continue on to Afghanistan on his own, while Pei Xingjian headed back to Chang'an to deliver his captive to Gaozong.[157] One of Pei's subordinates was appointed protector-general of Anxi and stayed behind with a military detachment to construct a heavily fortified outpost at Suyab (Ak-Beshim, near modern Tokmok, Krygyzstan), a Sogdian trading post and former Western Türk capital. He then used Suyab as a base for monitoring the Western Türks, who again revolted in 682 and were promptly quelled.[158]

By the time Pei Xingjian returned to Chang'an in triumph, a major revolt had broken out among the Eastern Türks of Inner Mongolia, growing to a strength of several hundred thousand. The causes of this revolt are unclear, but a much later Old Turkic runic inscription from 731, composed on behalf of the Eastern Türk khagan of the time, claims that his people finally tired of being made to fight the Tang emperor's wars and longed to regain their independence:

> The chiefs of the Türks gave up their Türk titles and those who went over to the Tabgach [Chinese] held Tabgach titles, obeyed the Tabgach khagan, and served him for fifty years.[159] For the Tabgach, they went on military campaigns against the khagan of Bükli [Goguryeo] far in the east, where the sun rises, and in the west as far as the Iron Gates.[160] They offered up their state and laws to the Tabgach khagan. However, the common people of the Türks said: "We used to be a people with an independent state. But where is our state now? For whose state are we fighting?" "We used to be a people with our own khagan. But where is our khagan now? Which khagan are we serving?" Having said that, they turned hostile against the Tabgach khagan.[161]

---

[157] Narseh did manage to return to Tokharistan, but his following gradually dwindled to several thousand. Tang records state that he traveled to Chang'an again twenty years later (708–9), was given an honorary command in the imperial guards, and died there of an illness at an unspecified date. *ZZTJ* 202.6390–92; *XTS* 221b.6259.

[158] *ZZTJ* 202.6392, 203.6407, 6409. There has been some debate over whether the Suyab outpost was located at Ak-Beshim or near Agni or Hami (Yiwu). I find the Ak-Beshim theory more persuasive. See Shang, "Tang Suiye yu Anxi sizhen."

[159] The early twentieth-century Sinologists Shiratori Kurakichi and Paul Pelliot read *Tabgach*, the name with which the Turkic peoples referred to the Chinese empire, as derived from Tuoba, the clan name of the Serbi (Xianbei) rulers of the Northern Wei dynasty (386/399–534). The original Serbi-language form might have been *Tagbach*. The Shiratori–Pelliot theory has become widely accepted among Western and Japanese academics. But other etymologies for *Tabgach* have been proposed during the last century, including *Tangjia* (House of Tang) and *Da Han* (Great Han), and these are often favored by Chinese scholars. See, for example, Zhang, "On the Origin of *Taugast*."

[160] The Iron Gate (*Temir kapig* in Old Turkic) was a mountain pass in Central Asia between Samarkand and Balkh.

[161] Translation adapted from Tekin, *A Grammar of Orkhon Turkic*, 261–73. I have also consulted the new translation in Chen, *A History of the Second Türk Empire*, 199.

Jonathan Skaff recently proposed a different explanation: Drought and exceptionally cold weather in north China in the late 670s may have killed many of the Eastern Türks' livestock and reduced them to starvation, fueling discontent.[162] Another factor may have been resentment at the ethnic prejudice and discrimination that the Eastern Türk elite still faced despite having served the Tang dependably for decades. In 670, for instance, Gaozong issued an edict recruiting the sons of Eastern Türk chiefs to serve as attendants to his heir apparent, but rescinded it after a court official objected that the sons of felt-wearing barbarians could only exert harmful moral influence on the future emperor.[163]

The Eastern Türk revolt was twice effectively decapitated by the capture of its leaders in 680–1, both times at the hands of armies under Pei Xingjian. But after Pei's death in 682, the revolt finally succeeded under Ashina Qutlugh (Gudulu, r. 682–92), who titled himself Ilterish Khagan. In 685–7, an anti-Tang revolt among the eastern Tegreg forced the Tang to relocate the headquarters of the Anbei Protectorate from central Mongolia to the Gansu Corridor. This gave Ilterish an opportunity to move his base of operations from the Inner Mongolian frontier to the Orkhon Valley, where his khaganate would be relatively invulnerable to Chinese attacks. As Türks began migrating to the steppe to join Ilterish in large numbers, the Tang attempted to counter his appeal by creating an alternative puppet khaganate under Ashina Gande (665–91), an imperial guard general and great-grandson of Illig Khagan.[164] Gande's untimely death in 691 put an end to that project. Ilterish himself died in 692 and was succeeded by his younger brother, who reigned as Kapaghan Khagan (r. 692–716) and brought the second Eastern Türk khaganate to the height of its power. Most of the eastern Tegreg peoples submitted to Kapaghan, but some, including at least one faction of the Uighurs, migrated to the Gansu Corridor and remained aligned with the Tang.[165]

Gaozong died in 683, after which Empress Wu first ruled through two of her sons (one of whom lasted less than two months before being deposed) and then took the throne herself at the age of 66. She reigned for fifteen years (690–705) as emperor of her own dynasty (the Zhou) before being forced to retire and restore the Tang dynasty to power.[166] Although Empress Wu's rise to become the only female emperor in Chinese history is often attributed to personal

---

[162] Skaff, *Sui-Tang China*, 273–74.

[163] *JTS* 190.4998; *XTS* 199.5661; *ZZTJ* 201.6363. The heir apparent at this time was Li Hong (652–675), who died young and therefore did not, in fact, succeed Gaozong.

[164] Zhao, "Tang Ashina Gande muzhi."   [165] *ZZTJ* 213.6779.

[166] Her original given name is unknown; after becoming emperor, she adopted the name Zhao, written with a newly created character. She was given various posthumous titles, including Great Sagely Empress Zetian; Chinese historians generally call her Wu Zetian. This essay will consistently call her Empress Wu and will refer to the empire during her reign as the Tang/Zhou. Note, however, that in 690–705 she was known by the same title *huangdi* that male emperors used.

political ambition, it is likely that she was also driven by a belief that the empire needed competent and experienced leadership in a fluid and challenging geopolitical environment. Her sons were politically inexperienced and easily manipulated, whereas she was strong-willed and had played an active role in court politics for over two decades, despite disapproval by Gaozong's ministers of a woman involving herself in such matters.

Empress Wu's response to the empire's frontier crises focused on regaining dominance over both the Tarim Basin and the Western Türks in order to contain Tibetan expansion into Central Asia and take pressure off the Qinghai front. Accordingly, Tang military forces began campaigning into the northern Tarim Basin from Xizhou in the late 680s. The first major offensive began in 686 but failed in 689 when a Tibetan counterattack, heavy snow, and logistical problems forced the Tang army to retreat.[167] A second offensive in 692 achieved complete success under a general who had spent years as a prisoner of the Tibetans and understood their tactics.[168] The Tang/Zhou moved the Anxi Protectorate back to Kucha and reestablished the Four Garrisons, though Suyab now replaced Agni as one of the four due to its importance in managing the Western Türks.[169] The new Four Garrisons boasted a total complement of 24,000 to 30,000 elite troops who had to be deployed from the imperial heartland and supplied with clothing and grain across the Taklamakan Desert, a heavy burden on imperial finances.[170]

Retaking the Tarim Basin was the only significant military success of Empress Wu's reign. Her policy toward the Western Türks was considerably less effective, being based on the same indirect rule strategy that had failed in the 660s. In fairness, it would have been unsustainably costly to expand the Chinese military presence in the western Turkic lands beyond Suyab while also maintaining the Four Garrisons. In the 690s and early 700s, both the Tang/Zhou and the Tibetans made efforts to exert influence over the ten tribes through client khagans, usually descendants of previous khagans from the Ashina lineage. These efforts were consistently unsuccessful, as the client candidates lacked local support and were rightly seen by their prospective subjects as puppets

---

[167] *ZZTJ* 203.6435, 204.6459; *THY* 73.1328.

[168] *ZZTJ* 205.6487–88; *XTS* 111.4148. Some Japanese and Chinese historians have argued that the Tang reconquered the Tarim Basin in 679 but pulled out in 686: see Shang, "Tang Suiye yu Anxi sizhen," 46–53, and the earlier studies cited therein. I believe the evidence better supports a limited raid by Tang forces from Suyab around 679 and an unsuccessful invasion in 686–9, followed by successful reconquest in 692. On this I essentially agree with Beckwith, *The Tibetan Empire*, 197–202.

[169] *THY* 73.1326.

[170] *JTS* 198.5304; *ZZTJ* 215.6847. In the 710s, a policy of collecting tolls on Sogdian merchants passing through the Tarim Basin was introduced to subsidize the Four Garrisons: *XTS* 221a.6230, 221b.6265.

serving outside forces. By 700, a non-Ashina tribe called the Türgesh (Ch. Tujishi) had established a new khaganate in the Ili River basin. They soon seized Suyab from its Tang/Zhou garrison and made it their capital.[171]

Empress Wu also faced new challenges in the north and northeast, both of which resulted in major setbacks. In 696, two *jimi* prefectures of the Mongolic-speaking Khitan people, who inhabited the Liao River basin, rebelled and overran the frontier area command of Yingzhou (Chaoyang, Liaoning). The Khitans slew Yingzhou's area commander, a Chinese official who had enraged them by treating their chiefs contemptuously "like slaves or servants" and refusing to provide relief grain during a famine. They lured a Tang/Zhou punitive expedition into an ambush and wiped it out, then began launching raids into Hebei for plunder and slaves.[172] The ambitious Kapaghan Khagan offered to attack the Khitans for Empress Wu in exchange for a marriage alliance in which his daughter would marry a Tang prince; he also requested various gifts including large quantities of grain seeds, silk, farming implements, and iron, as well as several thousand Eastern Türk families still living on Tang territory.[173] Empress Wu initially rejected these terms, but finally accepted them in 697 after the Khitans destroyed another Tang/Zhou army. Kapaghan then raided the Khitans' home base and captured their plunder and family members while their best warriors were out raiding Hebei. Upon receiving news of this, the Khitan army routed in panic and was destroyed by Tang/Zhou forces. However, rather than submit again to Tang/Zhou suzerainty, the Khitans became Kapaghan Khagan's vassals and remained so until his death (in an ambush by Tegreg rebels) in 716. Yingzhou thus stayed in Khitan hands for the next twenty years, since a Tang/Zhou attempt at recapturing it would have risked war with the Eastern Türks.

The Tang/Zhou partnership with Kapaghan proved extremely fleeting. Even though Empress Wu had replaced the Tang with her own dynasty, Kapaghan refused to recognize her clan as legitimate royalty and took offense when the prince who arrived to marry his daughter in 698 turned out to be the female emperor's grand-nephew Wu Yanxiu (d. 710), rather than a member of the Tang imperial clan. Kapaghan also claimed that the gifts he had received were of poor

---

[171] *ZZTJ* 206.6540, 207.6563.   [172] *ZZTJ* 205.6505–07, 6510.

[173] As noted earlier, Chinese marriage diplomacy always involved giving princesses to foreign rulers, not receiving princesses from them. Kapaghan's proposed marriage alliance would have made him the more powerful party in the relationship, as the father-in-law of a potential future emperor. The gift items requested were useful for creating an agrarian economy on the steppe (seeds and farming tools) or prized for their scarcity in nomadic society (silk and iron). The Eastern Türk families handed over to Kapaghan were previously distributed among six prefectures in the Ordos and north Shanxi. The *Zizhi tongjian* claims that they submitted to the Tang in 670–4, but since the Eastern Türk revolts had not yet begun at that time, they are more likely to have been Türks who did not head north to join Ilterish's new khaganate in the 680s. *ZZTJ* 205.6509–10; *XTS* 111.4148, 215a.6045.

quality. These complaints appear to have served mainly as a pretext for him to attack Hebei, a wealthy region whose weak defenses the Khitans had exposed. Kapaghan's pillaging of Hebei in the fall of 698 proved even more devastating than the Khitans' raids. Large Tang/Zhou conscript armies sent to intercept him dared not engage in battle and merely tailed his army from a distance, presumably due to their lack of cavalry. Indeed, in the aftermath of the Khitan and Eastern Türk raids, prefectures in Hebei and Henan began forming professional cavalry units for defense, a belated acknowledgment that the era of relying on Turkic peoples as military manpower was over for now.[174]

The damage done by the Khitan revolt led some Tang/Zhou officials to argue that the empire was still overextended even after sacrificing the conquests in Korea. In 696, the Tibetan empire had proposed peace via another marriage alliance, on the condition that the Tang/Zhou create a buffer zone in Central Asia by abolishing the Four Garrisons of Anxi and giving the Tibetans suzerainty over half of the Western Türk tribes. Empress Wu's court debated this proposal and ultimately rejected it.[175] But in 697, the minister Di Renjie (630–700) submitted memorials to recommend abolishing the Four Garrisons and handing the Tarim Basin over to the current Western Türk client khagan, in order to concentrate on defending the northern frontier. Di metaphorically described such retrenchment as nourishing the "Central Lands," which had been starved of resources for the sake of "fattening the barbarians." In the same spirit, Di Renjie suggested withdrawing Tang troops from the Andong Protectorate in Liaodong and handing it over to a descendant of the Goguryeo royal family.[176] Empress Wu rejected his proposal on the Four Garrisons but effectively adopted the proposal on Liaodong, as she downgraded the Andong Protectorate to an area command in 698 and appointed a son of the last Goguryeo king as area commander, effectively converting it into an autonomous *jimi* polity.[177] This decision seems to have been necessitated by the new Eastern Türk threat to Hebei and the Khitans' continued occupation of Yingzhou, which cut off land access to Liaodong from Hebei and meant that Tang/Zhou troops in Liaodong could only be supplied, rotated, and reinforced by sea. The Liaodong garrisons were probably all withdrawn by 700 and never reestablished, even after the Tang reoccupied Yingzhou in 717.[178]

Tang sources state that the Andong area command soon collapsed, as most of its "former Goguryeo households" left to join either the Eastern Türks or the

---

[174] *ZZTJ* 206.6530–35, 6539.　　[175] *ZZTJ* 205.6508–09; *TD* 190.5173–77.

[176] *ZZTJ* 206.6524–25; *THY* 73.1318–19, 1326–27; *CFYG* 991.11482.

[177] *XTS* 220.6198. The Andong Protectorate was revived in 705–61 but was continuously located in northeastern Hebei, not Liaodong, indicating that it no longer controlled Liaodong and was focused on *jimi* polities among the Khitan, *Qay (Xi), and Margat tribes.

[178] Yingzhou was lost to the Khitans again, this time permanently, during the An Lushan Rebellion of 755–63.

Margat.[179] In the immediate aftermath of the Khitan capture of Yingzhou and the Tang withdrawal from Liaodong, Margat groups joined hands with former Goguryeo subjects from Liaodong to establish a kingdom in the Changbai Mountains. This state came to be known as Bohai (Kor. Balhae/Parhae) after the official title, Prince of Bohai Commandery, that the Tang conferred on its ruler in 714. The title was upgraded to King in 762, a belated recognition of Bohai's independence, though Bohai also formally remained an area command within the *jimi* system.[180] Although Chinese and Korean historians have engaged in a politicized debate over the ethnicity of Bohai's ruling family, there seems to be little doubt that the majority of its population was Margat in origin, with Goguryeo immigrants as an influential minority.[181]

Bohai eventually expanded to the upper reaches of the Liao River and into the northernmost parts of the Korean peninsula, but it does not appear to ever have taken control of Liaodong or extended as far south as Pyongyang. An expanded buffer zone between the Tang, Silla, and Bohai, which now included Liaodong, served to prevent or at least minimize conflict between the three states.[182] But the Tang tacitly allowed this zone to exist only because Empress Wu had decided, by the end of the seventh century, that the empire's strategic priorities lay in holding its northern and western frontiers against the Tibetan and Turkic threats. From a long-term perspective, therefore, the late seventh century's significance lay in the Tang empire permanently abandoning its claim to Liaodong and parts of the Korean peninsula and shifting to focus on holding its Central Asian protectorate. But the eighth century would end with the Tang losing that protectorate as well, as an indirect consequence of the An Lushan Rebellion (755–63). That story will be told in the sequel to this Element, titled *Late Tang China and the World*.[183]

---

[179] *JTS* 199a.5328. A Goguryeo refugee community among the Eastern Türks was still in existence in 715, when its leader (who had intermarried with Türk nobility) defected to the Tang during a revolt against Kapaghan Khagan: *ZZTJ* 211.6709; *CFYG* 964.11171. Chinese and Korean historians disagree over whether a viable "Lesser Goguryeo" state existed in Liaodong until the ninth century; in my opinion, Liaodong is more likely to have become a stateless zone.

[180] Kim, "Diplomatic Priorities," 8–11, 15–18.

[181] Given our uncertainty as to what language the Bohai elite spoke, I have chosen not to follow the Western academic convention of referring to it by the Korean reading of its Sinitic-derived name. Sloane, "Parhae in Historiography and Archaeology."

[182] Kim, "A Buffer Zone for Peace"; Yang, *Frontiers of the Tang and Song Empires*, Map 5, at https://storymaps.arcgis.com/stories/0cf7988787 45406fa5719b97ccfc5454#ref-n-YrNoOg. The only case of armed conflict between the three sides occurred in 732–3 when Bohai conducted a seaborne attack on a Tang naval base in Shandong, perhaps aiming to weaken Tang naval forces and thus preempt a seaborne invasion. The Tang responded by ordering Silla to mount a land invasion of Bohai, but the Silla army lost half its men in a snowstorm and retreated. See *JTS* 199b.5361; *XTS* 219.6180–81.

[183] Yang, *Late Tang China and the World*.

6 Southern Frontiers and Maritime Trade (to ca. 750)

While the Tang struggled to stabilize its overextended frontiers in the northeast and northwest, the southern frontiers remained relatively calm and free of geopolitical conflict during the seventh century. This is not to say that the south was perceived in an altogether positive light. Chinese migrants from the north had been moving into southern frontier areas for centuries, particularly the lower and middle Yangzi regions, the Sichuan Basin, and the Pearl River delta (Guangdong/Lingnan). In these regions, military support from the Chinese imperial state enabled northern colonists to drive the indigenous hunter-gatherer inhabitants into the hills, establish cities and towns, and begin cultivating rice intensively in the plains and river basins. By early Tang times, the lower Yangzi (Jiangnan) and the Sichuan Basin were seen as essentially civilized by Chinese settlement, albeit still somewhat exotic, while the middle Yangzi and areas further south were considered wilder and far less hospitable. In the eyes of the Tang political elite, who mostly originated from and resided in north China, the far south was a dangerous place of humid, miasmic (i.e., malarial) forests teeming with exotic plants and animals, as well as a confusing jumble of tribes and peoples who spoke strange languages, practiced black magic, and worshiped unfamiliar spirits.[184] It was a common destination for convicts sentenced to exile, as well as officials who had fallen out of imperial favor. The only posting in the far south that a Tang official might covet was to the port city of Guangzhou, for reasons explained below.

The Tang southern frontier extended as far south as the Jiaozhou area command, established at Hanoi in 624 to supervise both regular and *jimi* prefectures in north Vietnam; it was upgraded to an Annan (Pacifying the South) Protectorate in 679. However, as reflected by Taizong's refusal to attack Champa in 630, the Tang had no ambitions to expand its territorial control or military dominance further south than Annan, even though Champa's northern-most territories had once been a Han dynasty commandery called Rinan. The fate of the Sui expedition that sacked the Cham capital in 605 probably served as a cautionary tale against military adventurism in the tropics: After dividing the reconquered Rinan area into three commanderies, nearly half the Sui expeditionary force (including the commanding general) had perished from diseases during its return march.[185] While the Tang maintained a hands-off approach to Champa, the Cham in turn refrained from raiding Tang territory and concentrated on gaining wealth through maritime trade.[186]

---

[184] For a classic study of Tang perceptions of the south, see Schafer, *The Vermilion Bird.*

[185] *ZZTJ* 180.5616, 5619, 190.5965.

[186] Giang, "Diplomacy, Trade and Networks." The only recorded border clash between Tang and Cham armies took place in 809: the Cham suffered a crushing defeat and reportedly lost over

Tang officials on the southwestern frontier did gradually impose greater influence over the peoples of Yunnan, who were still too disorganized to create effective states.[187] A punitive expedition in 648, launched from Sichuan, drove all the way to Lake Erhai and forced seventy indigenous tribes into submission under the *jimi* system. Tang ethnographers noted that some local clans claimed to be descended from Chinese colonists and still resembled the Chinese in language and customs. Another armed expedition in 651 created more *jimi* polities in the Kunming area.[188] In 664 the Tang established Yaozhou area command, a remote outpost in modern Yao'an county (between Kunming and Dali), to oversee Yunnan's *jimi* polities. The area commander was a Chinese official with a garrison of 500 troops rotated annually from central Sichuan. By 698, it was known as a lawless haven for fugitives and vagrants from Sichuan, but the Tang court saw it as strategically useful for keeping Tibetan influence out of Yunnan and rejected calls to abolish it. Tang sources typically attribute occasional indigenous revolts in Yaozhou to Tibetan incitement, but the local officials' harsh and over-aggressive ways were as much to blame.[189] Interested in creating a counterweight to growing Tibetan political influence in Yunnan, Tang officials in Sichuan and Yaozhou sponsored the Nanzhao kingdom's rise as a client state in the 730s. But Tang efforts at reining in the second Nanzhao king's territorial ambitions led him to realign with the Tibetans and conquer Yaozhou in 750. In the ensuing frontier war (751–4), the Tang lost up to 200,000 troops, primarily to disease, in vain attempts at taking Nanzhao's capital (modern Dali).[190] Nanzhao would remain something of a wild card in Tang foreign relations, cannily maneuvering for advantage and security in the space between its more powerful neighbors.

Other parts of the southern frontier were characterized by greater stability but intermittent indigenous resistance to the imperial state. Unfortunately, there is much that we don't know about such indigenous revolts, due to their cursory treatment in records written by court historians who tended to view warfare on the southern frontiers as less important to the empire's security. In 687, the native people of Annan (whom the Chinese called *Li*) rebelled and killed the protector-general because he had abolished the customary law permitting them to pay half the regular tax rate. The rebels seized Hanoi but were soon put down by troops deployed from Guangxi.[191] The upland inhabitants of *jimi* polities in Sichuan,

---

30,000 men, along with an equivalent number of weapons, war canoes, and war elephants (*THY* 73.1321, 98.1751).

[187] Chinese ethnographic descriptions of these peoples can be found in *XTS* 222c.6315–22.

[188] *ZZTJ* 199.6255–56, 6276–78, 202.6368. See also Backus, *The Nan-chao Kingdom*, 3–23.

[189] *ZZTJ* 201.6340, 206.6537; *THY* 73.1330–32; Backus, *The Nan-chao Kingdom*, 30–40.

[190] Yang, *Frontiers of the Tang and Song Empires*, Map 6, 6c, at https://storymaps.arcgis.com/stories/0cf798878745406fa5719b97ccfc5454#ref-n-Ar2rKw.

[191] *ZZTJ* 204.6445.

Guizhou, Guangxi, and Guangdong, whom the Chinese variously labeled as *Man* or *Lao*, occasionally raided nearby Tang prefectures as well.[192] This was perhaps in reaction to encroachment and oppression by Chinese colonists, though Tang records almost never explain "rebel" motives.[193] Local officials responded with punitive expeditions that often returned with thousands of captives to be sold as slaves. In the 720s, Li and Lao revolts in Annan, Guangdong, and Guangxi increased significantly in scale as native chiefs banded together to resist domination by the imperial state. Imperial armies responded with great brutality, massacring rebels in the tens of thousands and heaping their decapitated bodies into great mounds to terrorize the survivors.[194] We thus see the Tang imperial presence stimulating the beginnings of "secondary state formation" on these frontiers, but also then suppressing it via the wholesale extermination of local elites.

By the 600s, Guangzhou had been the main Chinese port for maritime trade with Southeast Asia and the Indian Ocean for about two centuries. The Chinese still lacked the shipbuilding and navigational skills for long-distance sea voyages; moreover, as mentioned earlier, Tang law forbade Chinese merchants to leave the country by either land or sea, forcing them into the passive role of waiting for foreign merchants or tribute missions to arrive. Consequently, maritime trade in the South China Sea was largely conducted by Southeast Asians, Indians, Sri Lankans, and Iranians, with Arabs joining in from the eighth century on.[195] Southeast Asian seagoing sailing ships, which the Chinese called Kunlun ships (*Kunlun bo*), were particularly known for their size and speed and appear to have dominated trade in these waters in the seventh and eighth centuries.[196] While the Tang Chinese applied the label *Kunlun* to various dark-skinned Southeast Asian peoples, including Chams, Khmers, and Malays, who were active maritime traders, many of the largest Kunlun ships would probably have been from the Sumatran Malay thalassocracy of Srivijaya, which is believed to have emerged as a major trading power around the mid-seventh century (Figure 6).[197] The Kunlun peoples also supplied slaves to the Chinese market who were renowned for their aquatic skills. Some slaves labeled

---

[192] For a good recent study of the Guangxi–Guangdong frontier, see Churchman, *The People between the Rivers*.

[193] A notable exception was a Lao revolt in Sichuan in 648, which broke out when local officials drafted the Lao to build ships for Taizong's planned second invasion of Goguryeo: *ZZTJ* 199.6258–59, 6261; *XTS* 222c.6327.

[194] Yang, "Letting the Troops Loose," 32–33; Churchman, *The People between the Rivers*, 192–93; Yang, *Frontiers of the Tang and Song Empires*, Map 6, 6f, at https://storymaps.arcgis.com/stories/0cf798878745406fa5719b97ccfc5454#ref-n-Ar2rKw.

[195] Heng, *Southeast Asian Interactions*, Sections 3 and 4; Wang, *The Nanhai Trade*.

[196] Manguin, "Trading Ships of the South China Sea," 255–64; Manguin, "Sewn Boats of Southeast Asia."

[197] Manguin, "Srivijaya."

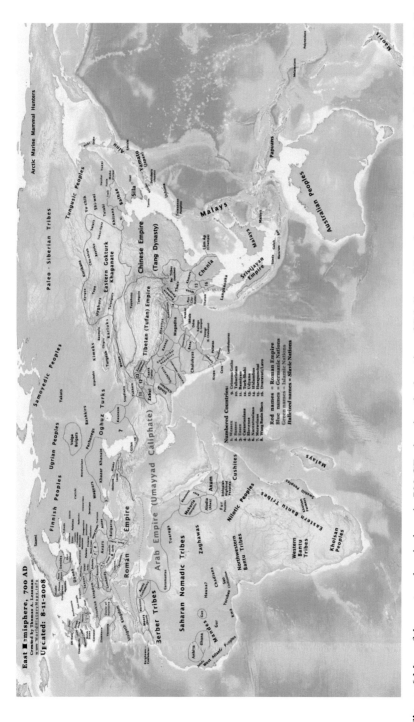

Figure 6 Map of the eastern hemisphere in 700 CE, showing the location of Srivijaya. Note that the map incorrectly depicts Bohai (Balhae) as controlling the Northeast Asian buffer zone. (Source: www.worldhistorymaps.info)

as *Kunlun* may in fact have been black East Africans imported by Arab or Iranian traders, who called them *Zanji* or *Zangi*.[198] According to Tang records, Srivijaya presented a female Zanji (*Sengqi* 僧耆/僧祇) slave to the Tang court as tribute in 724, along with two midgets, an orchestra, and a colorful parrot.[199]

The Chinese Buddhist monk Jianzhen (688–763), who briefly sojourned in Guangzhou in 748 after an attempt at sailing to Japan went awry, claimed to have seen "countless Brahmin [Poluomen, i.e., Indian], Persian [Bosi, i.e., Iranian], and Kunlun ships moored on the [Pearl] River, carrying aromatics and riches piled as high as mountains." Jianzhen learned that numerous foreign merchant communities resided in Guangzhou, including Sri Lankans and Arabs, and that the city had three Hindu temples staffed by Indian Brahmins.[200] Ten years later, an army of Arabs and Iranians apparently attacked the city of Guangzhou and looted and burned the port's warehouses before fleeing by sea.[201] Extant records provide no context that would enable us to identify the attackers' backgrounds and motivations. Some historians have theorized that they were not ordinary merchants but slave-soldiers in the service of a Chinese pirate lord named Feng Ruofang.[202] Feng was based on the island of Hainan, and we know of him only from an account of Jianzhen's encounter with him in 748:

> Feng Ruofang, a leading chief in the prefecture [of Wan'anzhou, on Hainan] invited [Jianzhen] to stay in his home and hosted him for three days. Every year, Ruofang captured two or three Persian ships, seized the goods on board and kept them for himself, and enslaved the crew. He had so many slaves that to see all of his slaves' homes, in one village after another, would take three days' travel on foot from north to south and five days on foot from east to west. When Ruofang entertained his guests, he always lit candles made of frankincense, using up more than a hundred *jin* of it at one go. In his backyard, sappanwood was piled up, like mountains, in the open air. His wealth in other commodities was of the same degree.[203]

While the Tang court saw the Southeast Asian region as strategically peripheral, it did have a strong interest in the same luxury imports from the South China Sea

---

[198] Wyatt, *The Blacks of Premodern China*, 18–20, 30–40.

[199] *CFYG* 979.11239; XTS 222b.9305. The text in the *Cefu yuangui* should be emended to read 僧耆 instead of *jiaqi* 價耆; cf. *CFYG* 972.11251 and *JTS* 197.5273, where Zanji slaves presented as tribute by Java (Heling 訶陵) in 815 and 818 are variously called *sengqi* 僧耆, *sengqi* 僧祇, and *jinqi* 金祇.

[200] Mabito Genkai, *Tō daiwajō tōseiden*, 74.

[201] *JTS* 198.5313; XTS 221b.6259; ZZTJ 220.7062.

[202] This theory originated with Edward Schafer in the 1960s: Schafer, *The Golden Peaches of Samarkand*, 16, 282–83 n. 77. Recent studies that adopt it include Chaffee, *The Muslim Merchants of Premodern China*, 12, 43–45; Liu and Zhang, "Tang Suzong nianjian."

[203] Mabito Genkai, *Tō daiwajō tōseiden*, 68. On the early history of Hainan as a part of the Chinese empire, see Schafer, *Shore of Pearls*.

and the Indian Ocean that Feng Ruofang regularly seized and enjoyed. Besides frankincense and aromatic woods like sappanwood, Tang elites also sought animal products like ivory, rhinoceros horn, and tortoiseshell. Such goods periodically arrived in Chang'an as tribute from Southeast Asian or South Asian states, but such was the imperial elite's appetite for them that the court also sought to monopolize access to them via trade. An edict from 661 instructs officials in the southern ports to prepare an annual shopping list of imported items for the imperial household's use and buy up the goods on it within ten days of a foreign merchant ship's arrival. Only then would the local people be allowed to buy the remaining goods.[204] In practice, however, the administration of maritime trade at Guangzhou was often much more corrupt and rapacious, despite periodic attempts at cleaning it up. The root of the problem was the government's monopoly on high-value foreign commodities, which forbade Chinese merchants and consumers to purchase these commodities directly from foreign traders, forcing them to pay marked-up prices to the state. This policy, effectively the inverse of the embargo on export of high-value Chinese goods like silk, was easily abused for personal profit by officials charged with enforcing it. Officials posted to Guangzhou frequently used the opportunity to line their pockets – by extorting extra "taxes" (i.e., bribes) from foreign merchants, for example, or forcing them to sell their goods below market value so they could be resold for a bigger profit.[205] In 684, the Guangzhou area commander Lu Yuanrui routinely allowed his staff to confiscate valuable goods from incoming Kunlun merchant ships for their personal use. Lu was finally assassinated by an irate Kunlun who, according to one account, also slew more than ten other Tang personnel with his hidden blade before escaping to sea.[206]

7 Tang China and the Buddhist World (to ca. 750)

Besides serving as an entrepôt for goods from the Indian Ocean and other parts of Southeast Asia, Srivijaya was also a Buddhist kingdom, making it a hospitable stopover for Buddhist monks traveling between China and India by sea. In 671, the Chinese Buddhist monk Yijing (635–713) sailed from Guangzhou to Srivijaya on board a ship owned by an Iranian (Bosi) and spent six months there, waiting for the monsoon winds to change so he could continue westward. He sailed to Bengal on another ship belonging to the Srivijayan king, then traveled on foot to the Buddhist monastic university of Nalanda, where he spent ten years learning how to read Sanskrit sutras and translate them into Chinese. Yijing left India with

---

[204] *THY* 66.1156.

[205] Officials posted in Guangzhou under pre-Tang dynasties had already engaged in such profiteering.

[206] *JTS* 89.2897; *XTS* 116.4223; *ZZTJ* 203.6420.

hundreds of hitherto-untranslated sutras, deposited them in Srivijaya, then returned to Guangzhou to procure a large supply of ink and paper. With a few co-translators recruited from the monasteries of Guangzhou, he spent another five years translating sutras in Srivijaya. In 694, Yijing made his final return to China and was soon recruited into a sutra translation project sponsored by the pro-Buddhist Empress Wu. For the next ten years, he worked alongside monk-translators from India and Khotan to make more Buddhist knowledge available in Chinese.[207]

Buddhism was introduced to China by Central Asian missionaries and merchants in the first century CE and received state patronage from the fourth century on. From the fourth century through the eighth, state-sponsored translation projects, headed by Indian and Central Asian monks, made the Buddhist sutras increasingly accessible to educated Chinese elites. The spread of Sinographic literacy to the Korean kingdoms and then Japan during this period allowed the religion to gain a following among their elites as well, often after being introduced by monks accompanying diplomatic missions. As a religion that had adherents, monastic institutions, and royal patrons across South Asia, Southeast Asia, Central Asia, and East Asia by the beginning of the seventh century, Buddhism was a driver of transregional travel and cross-cultural exchange far beyond the Tang empire's land frontiers. After Sogdian, Indian, and Iranian merchants, Buddhist monks of various ethnicities were the other great travelers of the seventh century, with large numbers journeying across Asia for purposes of pilgrimage, study, and proselytization, and learning new languages along the way. An early example was the famous Xuanzang (ca. 602–64), who journeyed to India via Central Asia in 629–30, returned in 645 with more than 600 Sanskrit texts previously unavailable in China, and wrote an influential account of the countries he had seen.[208] Xuanzang and Yijing had exceptionally successful careers as translators after their travels ended, but their willingness to travel and sojourn abroad for extended periods was by no means exceptional among Buddhist clergy. During his time in Srivijaya, Yijing penned short biographies of about sixty other monks from the Tang and Silla who had, in recent years, journeyed to South Asia by land or sea or had perished in the attempt. He had met some of them and knew of the others by word of mouth.[209]

Monk-pilgrims were often accorded great hospitality and respect by local pro-Buddhist rulers, but the stories told by Yijing show that long-distance travel remained plagued by various dangers including shipwreck, bandits, and deadly

---

[207] Sen, "Yijing and the Buddhist Cosmopolis"; Yijing, *Da Tang xiyu qiufa gaoseng*, 152–54, 214–44, 261–64.

[208] Brose, *Xuanzang*.

[209] These biographies are found in Yijing, *Da Tang xiyu qiufa gaoseng*, 1–208.

diseases. Yijing himself was once robbed of his clothes on the road to Nalanda and, having heard stories that the local inhabitants sacrificed fair-skinned people to their gods, was forced to cover his naked body with mud as a kind of disguise.[210] Despite such perils, adventurous Chinese and Korean monks continued to seek passage to the land of the Buddha in the eighth century. One such was Hyecho (ca. 704–ca. 780), a young Sillan monk who went to China in the early 720s. In 724, he traveled the sea route from Guangzhou to India, where he visited sites of the Buddha's life. He returned to China via northeastern Iran and Central Asia in 727 and remained in Chang'an as a disciple of two eminent Indian masters of Esoteric or Tantric (Mantrayana/Vajrayana) Buddhism, a relatively new tradition that had recently been introduced from India and was gaining popularity among the Tang elite. Hyecho is believed to have stayed in China for the rest of his life.[211] His written description in Classical Chinese of the countries he visited was evidently modeled after Xuanzang's earlier account, but was lost for many centuries. An incomplete manuscript was rediscovered in a sealed cave in Dunhuang, Gansu, in 1900, along with many other previously lost texts from the Tang and Tibetan empires, including the *Old Tibetan Annals*.[212]

Apart from a single known case from the ninth century, Japanese monks did not attempt to travel to India.[213] But many did travel to China during the Sui and Tang, usually as members of official tribute missions.[214] This gave them access to sutras and doctrines unavailable in Japan, such as Esoteric rites, as well as the opportunity to interact with Chinese, Korean, and Indian co-religionists, study under Chinese Buddhist masters, and make pilgrimages to sacred sites of Chinese Buddhism – particularly Mount Wutai in Shanxi, which had become known throughout the Buddhist world as the abode of the Bodhisattva Mañjuśrī.[215] Japanese monks visiting China in the early eighth century were also interested in recruiting well-respected Chinese monks to relocate to Japan and teach at their monasteries. Among the monks who accepted such an invitation, the most influential were Daoxuan (Jp. Dōsen, 702–60) and Jianzhen (Jp. Ganjin), who arrived in Japan in 736 and 753 respectively and stayed for the rest of their lives. The ship on which Daoxuan traveled to Japan also carried the Indian Huayan (Avataṃsaka) Buddhist master Bodhisena (704–60), a Cham monk-musician,

---

[210] Ibid., 153.   [211] Lopez, *Hyecho's Journey*.

[212] On the library cave in Dunhuang, see Hansen, *The Silk Road*, 285–321. The cave contained Tibetan texts because Dunhuang, a Tang prefecture, was captured by the Tibetan empire in 786 and remained under Tibetan rule until 848

[213] This exception was Shinnyo (799–865?), the former Imperial Prince Takaoka, who set sail from Guangzhou in 865, after a period of study in Chang'an, but reportedly died from being mauled by a tiger during a stop in Southeast Asia.

[214] Bingenheimer, *A Biographical Dictionary of the Japanese Student-Monks*.

[215] On the origins of this association of Mount Wutai with Mañjuśrī, see Sen, *Buddhism, Diplomacy, and Trade*, 76–86.

and an Iranian physician, reflecting the extent of Japan's interest in importing skilled foreigners.[216]

The tale of Jianzhen's persistence in trying to get to Japan, despite repeated failures, is told in a vivid account of his trials and tribulations by the Japanese literatus Ōmi no Mifune (also known by the Buddhist name Genkai, 722–85).[217] Due to the Tang empire's strict controls on private foreign trade and cross-border travel, even monks could face formidable challenges in obtaining permission to leave the country without support from patrons within the government.[218] Jianzhen was arrested in 744 after other monks (including one of his disciples) informed the authorities in Yangzhou of his plans to travel to Japan. On three other occasions, Jianzhen was able to set sail illegally without being discovered and stopped, only to be wrecked or blown badly off course; he lost his eyesight from an infection during one of these attempts. He was finally smuggled out with a returning Japanese embassy in 753, after the pro-Daoist emperor Xuanzong (Li Longji, r. 712–56) refused to approve that embassy's petition to take him to the Japanese court and insisted that Daoist priests be sent to Japan instead. It was such religiously motivated determination in successive generations of traveling monks (both Chinese and Japanese), rather than court-to-court diplomatic interactions alone, that helped make Buddhism a core element of Japanese imperial ideology and aristocratic culture during the Nara (710–94) and Heian (794–1185) periods.

Conclusion: Thinking Critically and Globally about the "Cosmopolitan" Tang

In recent decades, the idea of cosmopolitanism has taken on a highly positive connection with globalization, diversity, inclusion, pluralism, and tolerance in Western academia. It has thus come to serve as the basis for a philosophical or ethical ideal of global citizenship that embraces the post-Cold War "liberal international order" while rejecting the influence of ultranationalism, religious bigotry, nativism, and racism. Western historians with liberal or multiculturalist leanings tend to think of themselves as cosmopolitan, or at least aspire to be so, and to prefer living in hyperdiverse and heavily globalized (thus "cosmopolitan")

---

[216] Wong, *Buddhist Pilgrim-Monks*, 110, 225.

[217] Mabito Genkai, *Tō daiwajō tōseiden*. Jianzhen's life and career are also analyzed (with a focus on Buddhist visual and material culture) in Wong, *Buddhist Pilgrim-Monks*, 221–50.

[218] In 671, Yijing had sailed from Guangzhou through the endorsement and financial sponsorship of the local official Feng Xiaoquan and his brothers. It is likely that the other monks of whose voyages he knew had traveled under similar official patronage. Another Chinese monk whom Yijing met in Srivijaya during his return voyage had come with an official Tang embassy in 683 and stayed on afterwards. See Yijing, *Da Tang xiyu qiufa gaoseng,*152, 207.

cities. This has made it difficult for them to resist idealizing the "cosmopolitan" elites and urban centers of historical empires that they have chosen to study, without subjecting their understanding of cosmopolitanism to much analytical rigor or scrutiny.[219] In effect, many historians seem to be assuming that an empire (especially a premodern, non-Western empire) can't be entirely bad if its imperialism is "cosmopolitan," because cosmopolitanism is an unequivocally good thing and they, too, are cosmopolitan liberals. Therefore, rather than praising premodern empires as great on the basis of their military power and territorial conquests (as was the norm for much of the twentieth century), historians who admire them for whatever reason tend now to glamorize them as engines of cross-cultural exchange and global trade – that is, as agents of early globalization. The Tang empire's close association with the frequently romanticized modern idea of the Silk Road has made it a perfect candidate for such glamorization.

Glamorization and overidealization of the Tang is, of course, not a solely Western phenomenon. An interpretation of the Tang empire as "China's golden age" originated among Chinese nationalist historians in the early twentieth century, at a time when the long-held Confucian belief in an ancient golden age of enlightened governance by morally perfect sage-kings was finally being rejected as mythic and ahistorical. The new perspective on the Tang was rooted in Western-derived and rather un-Confucian views on what made an empire great: namely, factors such as territorial conquest and military might. The interpretation of the Tang as a golden age was suppressed as "rightist" in Maoist China, where the true golden age was believed to be in the socialist future rather than the dark "feudal" past, but it became entrenched in Western historiography and among Chinese communities outside the People's Republic (including those in Hong Kong and Taiwan). Reintroduced to the mainland in the 1980s, it has been increasingly politicized and promoted by the Communist regime, which has moved away from class-based denunciation of "feudal" imperial dynasties and re-embraced the country's imperial past as a locus of nationalist nostalgia and cultural pride. The "Great Tang" now features heavily in state propaganda surrounding the "Chinese Dream" ideology and the Belt and Road Initiative (billed as a revival of the Tang-era Silk Road), as well as Chinese political discourse on the ideal of a revived Sinocentric world order.[220]

This ironic use of the idea of cosmopolitanism to promote Chinese nationalism and Sinocentrism is not the whole story, however. China's increasingly repressed and isolated liberal intellectuals are also drawn to the popular image of the Tang as a utopian age of open-mindedness and intellectual pluralism,

---

[219] For a critique of this tendency, see Lavan *et al.* eds., *Cosmopolitanism and Empire*, 9–10.
[220] See Fong, "Imagining the Future from History."

embodied by its ubiquitous association with the modern Chinese terms *kaifang* ("openness"), *duoyuan* ("pluralism"), and *baorong* ("tolerance") and the older colloquial phrase *daqi* ("magnanimity"). Conservative nationalists see early Tang society's fabled openness to foreigners and foreign cultures as a *product* of the supreme self-confidence and security afforded by military power and wealth: A strong China can afford to be open *on its own terms*, while a weak China cannot. The liberals, however, would prefer to credit the empire's greatness and strength to its openness itself and use the Tang ideal to argue for more pluralism, freedom, and receptivity to Western liberal ideals in today's censorship-obsessed China. In other words, conservatives and liberals may disagree over what kind of political culture their country should have, but they share common ground in viewing the Tang, and the early Tang in particular, as a model and precedent for it. Such is the power and appeal of the "golden age" mythos.

Both Western and Chinese treatments of Tang "cosmopolitanism" thus tend to indulge in a kind of presentism that oversimplifies, sanitizes, and romanticizes the Tang, as is generally the case with any historical era nostalgically elevated as a country or civilization's golden age. Thinking more comparatively and globally might alert us to the fact that the existence of significant ethnic and cultural diversity, or of openness to foreign cultures, does not make an empire inherently more benign or enlightened than an ethnic nation-state. After all, empires by their very nature are built on military conquest and domination of other peoples, and frequently engage in selective appropriation of the conquered peoples' "exotic" cultural practices or material cultures in a way designed to symbolize their subjecthood and enhance the imperial elite's prestige. As I have argued elsewhere, every empire's "cosmopolitan" character has a darker side of oppression and violence that is usually most visible at its unstable, ambiguous, and heavily militarized edges, not at its political and cultural center.[221] We too often forget that the Tang was no exception to this rule, and that its aspirations and pretensions to geopolitical preeminence and universal hegemony rarely went unchallenged by its "barbarian" neighbors. The empire therefore constantly had to assert and maintain its supremacy on various frontiers at great cost in blood and treasure, a cost paid not by officials and their families (who were exempted from taxes and conscription) but by the longsuffering peasantry, for whom life was never all that "golden." And the cost in "barbarian" lives could be heavy too: Throughout the dynasty's history, victorious Tang armies were known to pillage "rebel" cities and massacre or enslave their inhabitants in

---

[221] Yang, "Letting the Troops Loose," 40.

a manner that the Han Chinese of today tend to assume was practiced only by "barbaric" Mongol, Manchu, and Japanese invaders.[222]

Contrary to the popular notion of "openness" being the key attribute of a "cosmopolitan" empire, the Tang state more often sought to control and restrict human movement within and across its borders than to remove barriers to such movement. Rather than promoting and protecting private foreign trade, as popular accounts of the Silk Road now claim, the Tang emperors criminalized such commerce (with the exception of a special category of expatriate Sogdian merchants) and even forbade their subjects to travel beyond the empire's frontiers on non-official business. Tang law also forbade marriages between Tang subjects (of any ethnicity) and subjects of other states (known legally as *huawairen*, "people from beyond the bounds of civilization"), except in the case of foreign envoys granted an extended stay in Chang'an – and even these were forbidden to take their Tang-subject wives back to their home countries.[223] Such laws meant that despite the empire's ethnic diversity, the non-elite population's ability to interact with the people of other states and empires in Eurasia was highly circumscribed, with consequent limits on the potential for cross-cultural exchange beyond the confines of the imperial court.[224]

If we understand a cosmopolitan individual as one who has gained the ability to cross cultural boundaries with relative ease, then the most important representatives and vectors of "cosmopolitanism" in the medieval Eurasian world to which the Tang belonged would have been traveling monks, merchants, students, and migrants of various ethnicities who were able to cross borders and bridge cultures despite these state-imposed restrictions. The monks Xuanzang, Yijing, Hyecho, and Jianzhen would belong in this category, as would men like Kibir Garik and Takamuko no Genri. Their cosmopolitanism would have been of a much deeper kind than that of emperors and aristocrats treating foreign objects, foodways, and fashions mostly as symbols of wealth and social prestige. Tang emperors from Taizong to Xuanzong may have enjoyed styling themselves as Celestial Khagans when addressing the peoples of the Inner Asian steppe, but their understanding of the Turkic languages and cultures was probably little better than that of their officials. The Tang ruling elite did have a taste for the Iranian game of polo and for the musical arts of Central Asia, both of which had been transmitted to China by the Sogdians during earlier dynasties.[225] But their engagement with Iranian and Central Asian culture was

---

[222] Yang, "Letting the Troops Loose."   [223] *TLSY* 8.178; *THY* 100.1796.

[224] For more on this subject, see Yang. "Unauthorized Exchanges."

[225] For a detailed exploration of Central Asian music in the Tang, see Currie and Christensen, *Eurasian Musical Journeys*, Sections 2 to 4. On polo, see Xiang, *Tangdai Chang'an yu xiyu wenming*, 111–24.

otherwise superficial, and relatively few ever traveled beyond the Sinitic heartland that they regarded as the center of the world's only civilization. Our sources
suggest that with rare exceptions like Li Chengqian, they generally regarded
most other cultures on the empire's periphery with indifference or condescen-
sion at best and revulsion at worst, valuing them only as a source of exotic
curiosities, luxury imports, fighting men, and slaves. In this, they were little
different from eighteenth-century European elites who drank tea and indulged
in chinoiserie as a form of conspicuous consumption.

The vast majority of extant texts from the Tang naturally reflect a Chang'an-
centered perspective, since they were written by officials and literati whose
worlds did revolve around the imperial capital.[226] As a result, we have a much
deeper understanding of elite life in Chang'an than for any other locality in the
Tang empire. But the absence of a similarly rich base of written sources from the
empire's non-metropolitan and subaltern subjects, foreign vassals and allies,
and internal and external enemies means that historians have to make a special
effort to understand *their* perspective and experience – for example, by reading
Sinocentric and court-centered sources against the grain, noticing and critiquing
the biases in their worldview rather than assuming that it adequately reflects
reality. In other words, one can better understand the Tang empire *as an empire*
by maintaining some emotional and critical distance from the Chang'an elite
and not empathizing or identifying exclusively with their point of view. By the
same token, I would suggest that we can understand the phenomenon of Tang
"cosmopolitanism" more critically and holistically by broadening our perspective beyond the culture, tastes, and worldview of the Chang'an imperial elite
and situating it within a global historical context rather than one defined by
either Western Sinology or modern Chinese national identity.

Such a holistic approach would see Tang "cosmopolitanism" not as centered
on, and emanating from, the reputed cosmopolis of Chang'an and the exotic
tastes of its elite denizens, but rather as a product of the whole empire's
interactions with a complex constellation of large, overlapping cultural, religious, and economic spheres or "cosmopoleis." At least two of these spheres
were a direct product of other projects of imperial conquest and expansion: the
Turkic world of the steppes, which stretched from Mongolia to the Volga and the
Caucasus; and the Islamic world, which emerged concurrently with the Tang
empire and by 750 extended from Spain and Morocco in the west to Sogdiana
and Sindh in the east. But there were also spheres of cosmopolitanism that either

---

[226] Manuscripts recovered from Dunhuang and Turfan, on the empire's northwestern frontier, are
the main exception. They have survived due to the dry conditions in that region and have
enriched our understanding of life on the empire's northwestern frontiers, though many were
still produced by local officials and elites. See Hansen, *The Silk Road*, 141–75, 285–321.

"emerged without empire" or extended beyond and between empires.[227] One important sphere in the latter category was the pre-Islamic Iranian world, which included the Sassanian empire and the states of Sogdiana before their fall to the Muslims, but also the Sogdian merchant networks and immigrant diasporas that dominated Central Asian trade and extended deep into the Sinitic and Turkic heartlands from the sixth century to the ninth. In recent decades, archaeological discoveries and new research have given us a better understanding of the scale of the Sogdian presence in Inner Asia and China during these centuries, as well as its role as a carrier of aesthetic and religious cultures from the pre-Islamic Iranian civilizational sphere to the Sinitic and Turkic worlds.

The constellation of cosmopoleis also included the increasingly interconnected Indian Ocean world of maritime trade routes, ports, and networks. This Indian Ocean world overlapped with much of the "Sanskrit cosmopolis" proposed by Sheldon Pollock, in which South Asian and Southeast Asian elites used classical Sanskrit literature (transcribed using a variety of Indic writing systems) as a common source of political and social capital from circa 300 CE to circa 1300 CE.[228] The Tang's engagement with this "Sanskrit cosmopolitan order" was minimal to nonexistent; only a relatively small number of Tang subjects (mostly monks like Xuanzang and Yijing) mastered the Sanskrit language, either when traveling to India on Buddhist pilgrimage or by learning from Indian monks in China.[229] And they used literacy in Sanskrit purely for reading and translating Buddhist sutras, not works like the *Ramayana*. But, as we have seen above, even this limited engagement with Sanskrit allowed the Tang to participate in a larger Buddhist world or "Buddhist cosmopolis," in which traveling Buddhist monks (and the scriptures they carried and translated) used the Sogdian and Indian Ocean routes to connect religious communities within a space spanning from India, Tibet, and the Tarim Basin to Korea and Japan.[230]

Finally, a "Sinographic cosmopolis" or Sinographic sphere emerged in East Asia from the seventh to ninth centuries, not so much as a product of Tang imperial expansion but rather as an outcome of state-building and political centralization in states that successfully resisted or escaped incorporation into the Tang empire while remaining within the Chinese tributary orbit.[231] Besides using Sinographic writing as a kind of "scripta franca," countries within the Sinographic sphere also tended to share political ideologies and institutions

---

[227] Quoting a phrase from Lavan *et al.* eds., *Cosmopolitanism and Empire*, 12.
[228] Pollock, *The Language of the Gods*.
[229] Kotyk, "The Study of Sanskrit in Medieval East Asia."
[230] For the term "Buddhist cosmopolis" see Sen, "Yijing and the Buddhist Cosmopolis."
[231] This sphere is known by numerous other names, including the East Asian cultural sphere, the kanji cultural sphere, and the Sinosphere. The Pollock-inspired term "Sinographic cosmopolis" was proposed by Ross King: see King, "Ditching 'Diglossia.'"

derived from the Tang imperial model, including state patronage of Buddhism and study of the Confucian classics.[232] Due to the popularity of the Silk Road image and the emphasis on openness and multiculturalism, historians have tended to take cultural influences from the Turkic, Iranian, and Islamic worlds as the benchmark for a "cosmopolitan" Chinese empire. But we should recognize Sinographic cosmopolitanism, in which Chinese cultural influence flowed outward, as equally deserving of the label "cosmopolitan." It certainly had a far more lasting impact on East Asian history. The history of the Sinographic sphere will be treated more fully in the sequel to this Element, *Late Tang China and the World*.

Historians of China have tended to privilege the Tang form of "cosmopolitanism" as though it were somehow exceptional in Chinese or world history, while ignoring the existence of other forms. We have also often fallen into the trap of crediting Tang "cosmopolitanism" to the attitudes of emperors and elites rather than the contributions of the people doing the actual traveling and trading. A more balanced view of the Tang empire's foreign connections can be gained by engaging more deeply with the histories and historiographies of other Eurasian regions and states, including new concepts of religious, linguistic, cultural, and literary cosmopolitanism that have emerged in recent years. Somewhat ironically, then, narratives of the "cosmopolitan" Tang must become less Sinocentric and parochial and acknowledge more fully China's place in a larger, interconnected, multicentered medieval world of numerous coexisting cosmopolitanisms.

---

[232] For the term "scripta franca" see Denecke, "Worlds Without Translation," 209.

Abbreviations

CFYG: Wang Qinruo 王欽若 *et al.*, *Cefu yuangui* 冊府元龜 [Outstanding Models from the Storehouse of Literature] (Nanjing: Fenghuang chubanshe, 2006).

JTS: Liu Xu 劉煦 *et al.*, *Jiu Tangshu* 舊唐書 [Old History of the Tang] (Beijing: Zhonghua shuju, 1975).

TD: Du You 杜佑, *Tongdian* 通典 [Comprehensive Institutions] (Beijing: Zhonghua shuju, 1988).

THY: Wang Pu 王溥, *Tang huiyao* 唐會要 [Institutional History of the Tang] (Taipei: Shijie shuju, 1968).

TLSY: Zhangsun Wuji 長孫無忌 *et al.*, *Tanglü shuyi* 唐律疏議 [The Tang Code with Commentaries] (Beijing: Zhonghua shuju, 1983).

XTS: Ouyang Xiu 歐陽修 *et al.*, *Xin Tangshu* 新唐書 [The New History of the Tang] (Beijing: Zhonghua shuju, 1975).

ZZTJ: Sima Guang 司馬光 *et al.*, *Zizhi tongjian* 資治通鑑 [Comprehensive Mirror to Aid Governance] (Beijing: Zhonghua shuju, 1956).

Bibliography

Arakawa Masaharu. "Aspects of Sogdian Trading Activities under the Western Turkic State and the Tang Empire," *Journal of Central Eurasian Studies* 2 (2011), 25–40.

Atwood, Christopher P. "Huns and Xiōngnú: New Thoughts on an Old Problem." In *Dubitando: Studies in History and Culture in Honor of Donald Ostrowski*, edited by Brian J. Boeck, Russell E. Martin, and Daniel Rowland (Bloomington, IN: Slavica Publishers, 2012), 27–52.

Atwood, Christopher P. "Some Early Inner Asian Terms Related to the Imperial Family and the Comitatus," *Central Asiatic Journal* 56 (2013), 49–86.

Backus, Charles. *The Nan-chao Kingdom and T'ang China's Southwestern Frontier* (Cambridge: Cambridge University Press, 1981).

Batten, Bruce L. "Foreign Threat and Domestic Reform: The Emergence of the Ritsuryō State," *Monumenta Nipponica* 41.2 (1986), 199–219.

Beckwith, Christopher I. *The Tibetan Empire in Central Asia* (Princeton, NJ: Princeton University Press, 1987).

Bi Bo 畢波. *Zhonggu Zhongguo de Sute Huren – yi Chang'an wei zhongxin* 中古中國的粟特胡人－以長安爲中心 [Sogdians in Medieval China: With Special Reference to the Sogdian Presence in the Capital Chang'an] (Zhongguo renmin daxue chubanshe, 2011).

Bingenheimer, Marcus. *A Biographical Dictionary of the Japanese Student-Monks of the Seventh and Early Eighth Centuries: Their Travels to China and Their Role in the Transmission of Buddhism* (Munich: Iudicium Verlag, 2001).

Brose, Benjamin. *Xuanzang: China's Legendary Pilgrim and Translator* (Boulder, CO: Shambhala, 2021).

Chaffee, John W. *The Muslim Merchants of Premodern China: The History of a Maritime Asian Trade Diaspora, 750–1400* (Cambridge: Cambridge University Press, 2018).

Chen, Sanping. *Multicultural China in the Early Middle Ages* (Philadelphia: University of Pennsylvania Press, 2012).

Chen Hao. *A History of the Second Türk Empire (ca. 682–745 AD)* (Leiden: Brill, 2021).

Chen Ken 陳懇. "Chile yu Tiele zuming xinzheng" 敕勒與鐵勒族名新證 [New Evidence on the Ethnonyms Chile and Tiele], *International Journal of Eurasian Studies* (*Ouya xuekan* 歐亞學刊) 11 (2022), 59–88.

Chu Chen-hung (Zhu Zhenhong) 朱振宏. *Sui Tang zhengzhi, zhidu yu duiwai guanxi* 隋唐政治、制度與對外關係 [Politics, Institutions, and Foreign Relations of the Sui and Tang] (Taipei: Wenjin chubanshe, 2010).

Churchman, Catherine. *The People between the Rivers: The Rise and Fall of a Bronze Drum Culture, 200–750 CE* (Lanham, MD: Rowman and Littlefield, 2016).

Currie, Gabriela, and Lars Christensen. *Eurasian Musical Journeys: Five Tales*, Elements in the Global Middle Ages (Cambridge: Cambridge University Press, 2022).

Denecke, Wiebke. "Worlds Without Translation: Premodern East Asia and the Power of Character Scripts." In *A Companion to Translation Studies*, edited by Sandra Bermann and Catherine Porter (Chichester, West Sussex: John Wiley & Sons, 2014), 204–16.

Dotson, Brandon. *The Old Tibetan Annals: An Annotated Translation of Tibet's First History* (Vienna: Verlag der osterreichischen Akademie der Wissenschaften, 2009).

Drompp, Michael. "Chinese 'Qaghans' Appointed by the Türks," *T'ang Studies* 25 (2007), 183–202.

Fong, Victor K. "Imagining the Future from History: The Tang Dynasty and the 'China Dream.'" In *Alternative Representations of the Past: The Politics of History in Modern China*, edited by Ying-kit Chan and Fei Chen (Berlin: Walter De Gruyter, 2021), 149–72.

Giang, Do Truong. "Diplomacy, Trade and Networks: Champa in the Asian Commercial Context (7th–10th Centuries)," *Moussons* 27 (2016), 59–82.

Graff, David A. *Medieval Chinese Warfare, 300–900* (London: Routledge, 2002).

Graff, David A. "Strategy and Contingency in the Tang Defeat of the Eastern Turks, 629–630." In *Warfare in Inner Asian History*, edited by Nicola Di Cosmo (Leiden: Brill, 2002), 33–72.

Hansen, Valerie. *The Silk Road: A New History with Documents* (Oxford: Oxford University Press, 2017).

Heng, Derek. *Southeast Asian Interactions: Geography, Networks, and Trade*, Elements in the Global Middle Ages (Cambridge: Cambridge University Press, 2022).

Holcombe, Charles. "Chinese Identity During the Age of Division, Sui, and Tang," *Journal of Chinese History* 4 (2020), 31–53.

Holcombe, Charles. "The Xianbei in Chinese History," *Early Medieval China* 19 (2013), 1–38.

Iwami Kiyohiro 石見清裕. *Tō no hoppō mondai to kokusai chitsujo* 唐の北方問題と国際秩序 [Northern Frontier Issues and International Order under the Tang] (Tokyo: Kyūko shoin, 1998).

Iwami Kiyohiro. "Turks and Sogdians in China during the T'ang Period," *Acta Asiatica* 94 (2008), 41–65.

Kao Ming-shih (Gao Mingshi) 高明士. *Dongya gudai de zhengzhi yu jiaoyu* 東亞古代的政治與教育 [Politics and Education in Ancient East Asia] (Taipei: Taiwan daxue chubanshe, 2004).

Kao Ming-shih (Gao Mingshi) 高明士 ed. *Tiansheng ling yizhu* 天聖令譯注 [The Tiansheng-Era Statutes with Translation and Commentary] (Taipei: Yuanzhao, 2017).

Kim Jong-bok. "A Buffer Zone for Peace: Andong Protectorate and Diplomatic Relations between Silla, Balhae, and Tang in the 8th to 10th Centuries," *Korea Journal* 54.3 (2014), 103–25.

Kim Jong-bok. "Diplomatic Priorities: Changes in the Tang Bestowal of Titles on Silla and Parhae," *Acta Koreana* 23.1 (2020), 1–22.

Kim Pu-sik 金富軾 (trans. and ann. Yi Pyŏng-do 李丙燾). *Samguk sagi* 三國史記 [Historical Records of the Three Kingdoms] (Seoul: Ŭryu munhwasa, 1983).

King, Ross. "Ditching 'Diglossia': Describing Ecologies of the Spoken and Inscribed in Pre-modern Korea," *Sungkyun Journal of East Asian Studies* 15.1 (2015), 1–19.

Kotyk, Jeffrey. "The Study of Sanskrit in Medieval East Asia: China and Japan," *Hualin International Journal of Buddhist Studies* 4.2 (2021), 240–73.

Lavan, Myles, Richard E. Payne, and John Weisweiler, eds. *Cosmopolitanism and Empire: Universal Rulers, Local Elites, and Cultural Integration in the Ancient Near East and Mediterranean* (Oxford: Oxford University Press, 2016).

Levi, Scott C. *The Bukharan Crisis: A Connected History of 18th-Century Central Asia* (Pittsburgh, PA: University of Pittsburgh Press, 2020).

Li Danjie 李丹婕. "Hanhai duhu fu yu Hanhai dudu fu zhi bian" 瀚海都護府與瀚海都督府之辨 [An Analysis of the Hanhai Protectorate and Hanhai Area Command], *Minzu yanjiu* 民族研究 6 (2019), 86–94.

Lin Kuan-Chun (Lin Guanqun) 林冠群. *Yubo gange: Tang-Fan guanxi shi yanjiu* 玉帛干戈: 唐蕃關係史研究 [Peace and War: Studies on Relations between the Tang and Tibetan Empires] (Taipei: Lianjing, 2016).

Lin, Shen-yu. "The Tibetan Image of Confucius," *Revue d'Etudes Tibétaines* 12 (2007), 105–29.

Liu Bao 劉寶 and Zhang Xiaogui 張小貴. "Tang Suzong nianjian 'Dashi Bosi tongkou Guangzhou' kao" 唐肅宗年間 "大食波斯同寇廣州" 考 [A Study of the 'Joint Arab-Persian Raid on Guangzhou' during Tang Suzong's Reign], *Jinan shixue* 暨南史學 11 (2015), 60–70.

Lopez, Donald S., Jr. *Hyecho's Journey: The World of Buddhism* (Chicago: University of Chicago Press, 2017).

Mabito Genkai 真人元開. *Tō daiwajō tōseiden* 唐大和上東征伝 [An Account of the Great Tang Monk's Journey to the East] (Beijing: Zhonghua shuju, 1979).

Manguin, Pierre-Yves. "Sewn Boats of Southeast Asia: The Stitched-Plank and Lashed-Lug Tradition," *International Journal of Nautical Archaeology* 48.2 (2019), 400–15.

Manguin, Pierre-Yves. "Srivijaya: Trade and Connectivity in the Pre-modern Malay World," *Journal of Urban Archaeology* 3 (2021), 87–100.

Manguin, Pierre-Yves. "Trading Ships of the South China Sea: Shipbuilding Techniques and Their Role in the History of the Development of Asian Trade Networks," *Journal of the Economic and Social History of the Orient* 36.3 (1993), 253–80.

Moriyasu Takao 森安孝夫. *Shirukurōdo to Tō teikoku* シルクロードと唐帝国 [The Silk Road and the Tang Empire] (Tokyo: Kodansha, 2016).

Pan, Yihong. "Locating Advantages: The Survival of the Tuyuhun State on the Edge, 300–ca. 580," *T'oung Pao* 99.4–5 (2013), 268–300.

Pollock, Sheldon. *The Language of the Gods in the World of Men: Sanskrit, Culture, and Power in Premodern India* (Berkeley: University of California Press, 2006).

Rothschild, N. Harry. *Wu Zhao: China's Only Woman Emperor* (New York: Pearson, 2008).

Schafer, Edward H. *The Golden Peaches of Samarkand: A Study of T'ang Exotics* (Berkeley: University of California Press, 1963).

Schafer, Edward H. *The Vermilion Bird: T'ang Images of the South* (Berkeley: University of California Press, 1967).

Schafer, Edward H. *Shore of Pearls: Hainan Island in Early Times* (Berkeley: University of California Press, 1970).

Sen, Tansen. *Buddhism, Diplomacy, and Trade: The Realignment of Sino-Indian Relations, 600–1400* (Honolulu: University of Hawaii Press, 2003).

Sen, Tansen. "Yijing and the Buddhist Cosmopolis of the Seventh Century." In *Texts and Transformations: Essays in Honor of the 75th Birthday of Victor H. Mair*, edited by Haun Saussy (Amherst, MA: Cambria Press, 2018), 345–68.

Shang Yongliang 尚永亮. "Tang Suiye yu Anxi sizhen bainian yanjiu shulun" 唐碎葉與安西四鎮百年研究述論 [A Survey of Research on Tang Suyab and the Four Garrisons of Anxi during the Past Hundred Years], *Zhejiang daxue xuebao* 46.1 (2016), 39–56.

Skaff, Jonathan Karam. *Sui-Tang China and Its Turco-Mongol Neighbors: Culture, Power, and Connections, 580–800* (Oxford: Oxford University Press, 2012).

Sloane, Jesse D. "Parhae in Historiography and Archaeology: International Debate and Prospects for Resolution," *Seoul Journal of Korean Studies* 27.1 (2014), 1–35.

Tekin, Talat. *A Grammar of Orkhon Turkic* (Bloomington, IN: Indiana University Press, 1968).

Wang Gungwu. *The Nanhai Trade: The Early History of Chinese Trade in the South China Sea* (Kuala Lumpur: Malayan Branch of the Royal Asiatic Society, 1958; rpt. Singapore: Times Academic Press, 1998).

Wang Wan-chun 王萬雋. "Nanchao de zuojun zuoxian" 南朝的左郡左縣 [The Peripheral Commanderies and Peripheral Counties of the Southern Dynasties], *Zaoqi Zhongguo yanjiu* 早期中國研究 11 (2019), 107–69.

Wang Xiaofu 王小甫. *Tang, Tufan, Dashi zhengzhi guanxi shi* 唐、吐蕃、大食政治關係史 [A History of Political Relations between the Tang, Tibetan, and Arab Empires] (Beijing: Beijing daxue chubanshe, 1992).

Wang, Zhenping. *Ambassadors from the Islands of Immortals: China-Japan Relations in the Han-Tang Period* (Honolulu: University of Hawaii Press, 2005).

Warner, Cameron David. "A Miscarriage of History: Wencheng Gongzhu and Sino-Tibetan Historiography," *Inner Asia* 13 (2011), 239–64.

Wei Zheng 魏徵 *et al. Suishu* 隋書 [History of the Sui] (Beijing: Zhonghua shuju, 1973).

Wong, Dorothy C. *Buddhist Pilgrim-Monks As Agents of Cultural and Artistic Transmission: The International Buddhist Art Style in East Asia, ca. 645–770* (Singapore: NUS Press, 2018).

Wu Jing (trans. Hilde de Weerdt, Glen Dudbridge, and Gabe van Beijeren). *The Essentials of Governance* (Cambridge: Cambridge University Press, 2020).

Wyatt, Don J. *The Blacks of Premodern China* (Philadelphia: University of Pennsylvania Press, 2010).

Xiang Da 向達. *Tangdai Chang'an yu xiyu wenming* 唐代長安與西域文明 [Tang Chang'an and the Civilization of the Western Regions] (Shanghai: Xuelin chubanshe, 2017 [1933]).

Xiong, Victor Cunrui. *Emperor Yang of the Sui Dynasty: His Life, Times, and Legacy* (Albany, NY: SUNY Press, 2005).

Yang, Shao-yun. "'What Do Barbarians Know of Gratitude?' The Stereotype of Barbarian Perfidy and Its Uses in Tang Foreign Policy Rhetoric," *Tang Studies* 31 (2013), 28–74.

Yang, Shao-yun. "Letting the Troops Loose: Pillage, Massacres, and Enslavement in Early Tang Warfare," *Journal of Chinese Military History* 6 (2017), 1–52.

Yang, Shao-yun. *Frontiers of the Tang and Song Empires* (StoryMap). First published online in 2020.

Yang, Shao-yun, *Late Tang China and the World, 750–907 CE*, Elements in the Global Middle Ages (Cambridge: Cambridge University Press, 2023).

Yang, Shao-yun. "Unauthorized Exchanges: Restrictions on Foreign Trade and Intermarriage in the Tang and Northern Song Empires," *T'oung Pao* 108 (2022), 588–645.

Yang, Shao-yun. "Tang 'Cosmopolitanism': Toward a Critical and Holistic Approach," *Modern Asian Studies* (forthcoming).

Yijing 義净. *Da Tang xiyu qiufa gaoseng zhuan jiaozhu* 大唐西域求法高僧傳校注 [Biographies of Eminent Monks of the Great Tang who Sought the Dharma in the Western Regions: An Annotated Critical Edition] (Beijing: Zhonghua shuju, 1988).

Zhang Feng. "Rethinking the 'Tribute System': Broadening the Conceptual Horizon of Historical East Asian Politics," *Chinese Journal of International Politics* 2 (2009), 545–74.

Zhang, Xushan. "On the Origin of *Taugast* in Theophylact Simocatta and the Later Sources," *Byzantion* 80 (2010), 485–501.

Zhao Zhenhua 趙振華. "Tang Ashina Gande muzhi kaoshi" 唐阿史那感德墓志考釋 [An Analysis of the Entombed Epitaph of Ashina Gande of the Tang], *Shilin* 史林 5 (2004), 82–87.

Acknowledgments

I would like to thank Geraldine Heng, Michael Höckelmann, Andrew Chittick, and two anonymous reviewers for their helpful comments on earlier drafts of this essay.

Cambridge Elements ≡

The Global Middle Ages

Geraldine Heng

University of Texas at Austin

Geraldine Heng is Perceval Professor of English and Comparative Literature at the University of Texas, Austin. She is the author of *The Invention of Race in the European Middle Ages* (2018) and *England and the Jews: How Religion and Violence Created the First Racial State in the West* (2018), both published by Cambridge University Press, as well as *Empire of Magic: Medieval Romance and the Politics of Cultural Fantasy* (2003, Columbia). She is the editor of *Teaching the Global Middle Ages* (2022, MLA), coedits the University of Pennsylvania Press series, RaceB4Race: Critical Studies of the Premodern, and is working on a new book, Early Globalisms: The Interconnected World, 500–1500 CE. Originally from Singapore, Heng is a Fellow of the Medieval Academy of America, a member of the Medievalists of Color, and Founder and Co-director, with Susan Noakes, of the Global Middle Ages Project: www.globalmiddleages.org.

Susan Noakes

University of Minnesota, Twin Cities

Susan Noakes is Professor and Chair of French and Italian at the University of Minnesota, Twin Cities. From 2002 to 2008 she was Director of the Center for Medieval Studies; she has also served as Director of Italian Studies, Director of the Center for Advanced Feminist Studies, and Associate Dean for Faculty in the College of Liberal Arts. Her publications include *The Comparative Perspective on Literature: Essays in Theory and Practice* (co-edited with Clayton Koelb, Cornell, 1988) and *Timely Reading: Between Exegesis and Interpretation* (Cornell, 1988), along with many articles and critical editions in several areas of French, Italian, and neo-Latin Studies. She is the Founder and Co-director, with Geraldine Heng, of the Global Middle Ages Project: www.globalmiddleages.org.

About the Series

Elements in the Global Middle Ages is a series of concise studies that introduce researchers and instructors to an uncentered, interconnected world, c. 500–1500 CE. Individual Elements focus on the globe's geographic zones, its natural and built environments, its cultures, societies, arts, technologies, peoples, ecosystems, and lifeworlds.

Cambridge Elements ☰

The Global Middle Ages

Printed in the United States
by Baker & Taylor Publisher Services